The Harlem I

Lessons Learned Along the

To Adam,

I wish you good health, peace, love and happiness (lesson 49)!

Thank you!!!

Wayne

The Harlem Line
Lessons Learned Along the Way

Cover design by J.W. Ford
Cover photograph by Yvonne C. Sobers

ISBN-13: 978-1717223586
ISBN-10: 1717223583

This book is dedicated to you, my

wonderful, loving and talented

granddaughters, Makala, Julia and Cayden.

I hope that it will inspire each of you

to excel in your endeavors, and

maximize your efforts and talents

in all that you do in your lifetime.

I love you!

Contents

Foreword

Officer. Gentleman. Meteorologist. Husband. Father. Award-winning sales executive. Entrepreneur. Teacher. Coach. Mentor. Leader.

Waynett A. Sobers has been all of these things and more during an extraordinary life of intrepidness, integrity, and excellence that began on February 15, 1937. While the tapestry of his story is woven with varied and rich experiences of every texture and emotional hue, there are common threads that are present throughout: those of opportunity, preparation, and risk. Mr. Sobers (he's cool with me calling him Wayne, but he'll always be Mr. Sobers to me) is making yet another valuable contribution as a mentor and role model by choosing now to write and release his memoir, *The Harlem Line*.

I had the pleasure of working with Mr. Sobers directly during my career as a member of the editorial staff of *Black Enterprise*, the iconic business magazine for African American achievers founded by the visionary Earl G. Graves. My first year at *Black Enterprise*, in 1987, when I was hired as an associate editor, was the last year of Mr. Sobers's first tour of duty at the magazine, in the role of executive vice president of Earl G. Graves Ltd. It was after that, when Mr. Sobers served as a member of *Black Enterprise*'s board of advisers and then became director of corporate communications in 1998, that I benefited the most from his guidance, mentorship, and example. By this time, I had risen to the position of vice president and editor in chief of *Black Enterprise*, serving alongside Mr. Sobers as a member of the company's senior management team.

But Mr. Sobers's influence on me began long before our overlapping tenures as employees of *Black Enterprise*. It began during my first year after graduating from Rutgers University in 1983, when I was editor in chief of Brooklyn, New York–based *Big Red News* (now the *New York Beacon*). The position, originally a temporary assignment, had just been made permanent by *Big Red News* publisher Walter Smith Jr. At the tender age of 24, I was running one of New York City's black newspapers, the one with the largest circulation at the time.

I had planned a special pullout section of the newspaper dedicated to the principles of Kwanzaa, the weeklong African American celebration of community and culture that takes place from December 26 through January 1. The editorial plan called for major profiles of black achievers who represented the essence of each of the Kwanzaa principles. One of my staffers, Geraldine Jones, pulled off a major coup, securing none other than Wayne Sobers, a top executive of *Black Enterprise*, for our profile representing *ujamaa*, or cooperative economics. It was then that I got my first exposure to Mr. Sobers, who had already established himself as a top performer in the media business as a top salesperson at Johnson Publishing Company (the Chicago-based publisher of *Ebony* and *Jet* magazines, where he worked before joining *Black Enterprise*) and as an inspirational role model. Little did I know that I would one day know him as a colleague, mentor, and friend—much less have the honor of being invited to write the foreword for his memoir.

If I shared all of the valuable lessons and advice Mr. Sobers has taught and continues to teach me, via both words and deeds, it could easily add a chapter or three to this book. But one valuable insight gifted to me by Mr. Sobers nearly two decades ago, during one of *Black Enterprise*'s annual company retreats, has served me particularly well during the highs, lows, and periods of turmoil and upheaval in my life.

Mr. Sobers told me about his most significant experience during his time working at the Equitable (now AXA Equitable Life Insurance Company), which resulted in what he calls "a philosophical attitudinal change" leading him to decide, "I refuse to have a bad day. I will not allow them!"

"I have lived by that mantra ever since," Mr. Sobers told me, "and discovered that all days are good, but some are just better than others! So, my advice to you, Alfred, is don't wait for outside conditions to determine whether your day will be good or bad. Decide that every day is a good day, and it will be."

I'd be lying if I said I understood and believed what Mr. Sobers was saying at the time. But eventually, as I endured trials, triumphs, adversity, and uncertainty in my own life, I eventually discovered that Mr. Sobers is absolutely right. Today, my wife, children, friends and family, and, most importantly, those I now mentor, know how I have embraced the every-day-is-a-good-day decision for my own life, via my daily mantra (and social media hash tag)—It's *good* to be me (#itsgoodtobeme)—regardless of external circumstances.

This book is a literal treasure chest of precious gems like this, just waiting to enrich your life and inspire you to not only reach, but exceed what you believe to be the limits of your potential. Ride with Mr. Sobers on *The Harlem Line*. It's a trip you'll never regret and won't soon forget.

—Alfred A. Edmond Jr.

Senior Vice President and Executive Editor at Large, Black Enterprise

Host of Money Matters, *American Urban Radio Networks*

Cocreator, Grown Zone Relationship Education at GrownZone.com

STATION: MORRISANIA

I was born in Morrisania Hospital on Monday, February 15, 1937, at about 5:00 a.m. My mother, Athlene A. Sobers, often said that I could have been born in Macy's on 34th Street. She had planned to go to Macy's on that day. If I had been born in the store, she'd say, she would probably have been gifted "six months of outfits from Macy's."

Mum (my grandmother Florence Sobers) had planned to take care of my sister, Jean, while my mother was in the hospital. In those days, women would stay in the hospital for about two weeks after giving birth. The day before I was born, my mother was preparing two weeks of clothes for Jean, who was almost five years old. Jean was "one slip [a female under garment] short of having fourteen complete sets" of clothes. My mother had planned to go to Macy's the next morning to get what she needed.

Early Monday morning, she woke my father and told him she'd had an unusual dream. She dreamt that I was born in the toilet and that I was bobbing up and down "dressed up like [the cartoon character] Tiny Tim." My father, shaken, told my mother not to get out of bed, and he ran to Mum's house, two blocks away, to tell her about the dream. When Mum heard the details of the dream, she commandeered a taxi, brought it to our house, put my parents in it, and ordered the driver to get my mother to the hospital post haste or else his clean cab was going to be a real mess.

My mother and I spent about ten days in Morrisania Hospital before we came home to 1516 Washington Avenue, between 171st Street, which separated the Morrisania and Tremont sections of the Bronx, and Claremont Parkway. That would be my home for twenty-six years.

STATION: CLAREMONT PARKWAY

In the late 1930s, New York City comprised neighborhoods divided by ethnic group. My neighborhood was unique because it had many ethnic groups: African American, Puerto Rican, Jewish, Irish, and Italian. There were few private houses. Most of the buildings were medium-size apartment buildings of ten to twenty apartments. But there were few buildings where any of these various ethnic groups lived in the same building.

Most of the apartments had windows facing Washington Avenue. Kids in the street always had adult eyes watching. So if you "messed up," you could count on your folks getting the word, and you knew your butt might be in jeopardy.

Washington Avenue, before the subway under the Grand Concourse was built, was the main north-south thoroughfare in the center of the Bronx. Most major parades took place there until the Grand Concourse was rebuilt.

I lived one block west of Third Avenue, where the Third Avenue elevated train (the Third Avenue El) ran, and one block east of Park Avenue. On Park Avenue, in an open cut below the street level, the Harlem Division of the New York Central Railroad and the New York, New Haven, and Hartford Railroad shared the four tracks from New York's Grand Central Station up to Woodlawn in the Bronx. After that station, the New Haven line switched to its own tracks to continue east to New England.

In the 1960s, the Metropolitan Transit Authority was formed and took over the commuter rail systems, buses, and most of the regional bridges and tunnels. The Harlem Division of the New York Central Railroad became the transit authority's Harlem Division, and the New York, New Haven, and Hartford Railroad became the New Haven Division.

I fell in love with trains. I loved to watch them, and even more, I loved to ride them. The Claremont Parkway station was two blocks from my house, and every chance I got, I would get somebody to take me to the station so I could watch the trains go roaring by, or to a local stop to pick up or discharge its passengers. My uncle Lewis, my father's younger brother, was my main target. I would plead with him to take me to watch the trains. He lived with us before he volunteered to join the US Army Air Corps soon after the attack on Pearl Harbor. My uncle Steve, my father's older brother, lived on Park Avenue adjacent to the Claremont Parkway station's northbound platform. Visiting him was always a treat. But that ended when he was drafted into the US Army at the commencement of World War II.

I learned a lot watching the trains. I learned how to identify the different locomotives each line used. The New Haven line had to use a larger locomotive that worked on both a third rail, which uses DC current, and a catenary (overhead) wire, which uses AC current. I learned the difference between third rails that were covered, to protect workers from being electrocuted, and those that were not, such as those that were used on the Third Avenue El. Making observations like these helped me become more knowledgeable.

Lesson Learned Along the Way

1. Being observant will heighten your awareness and ability to learn.

Growing Up on Washington Avenue

Where I lived on Washington Avenue, most of the three-to-five-story apartment buildings had wooden staircases and floors and had steel fire escapes that were usually in the rear or sides of the buildings, though a few were on the street side of the buildings. Many of the apartments were railroad flats—that is, each room was directly connected to the next room or connected through a short hallway. Privacy was rare. Because the buildings' interiors were primarily wood and plaster, they burned down in a hurry when there was a fire.

Because this was before we had smoke detectors, the best fire alarm was a dog sensitive to smoke. Our family security guard was Buddy, a Belgian Shepherd who became a legend because of the way he protected our family. Before his arrival, we had another dog called Chippy. Chippy was old when I was brought into our house. I was four years old when Mum brought Buddy to our house. Mum told us he had a little wolf in him, and from the way he could fight, we had no doubt she was right.

A short time after Buddy became a member of the family, we had Chippy euthanized because of her age. Chippy's disappearance changed Buddy's attitude toward other animals. He began to attack and be aggressive toward any animal within four feet. He was strong, and you would have to be alert when walking him near other animals. Outside the house, he was not aggressive toward people unless they appeared to threaten one of us. People in the neighborhood realized that and usually gave us a wide berth when we were walking him. If my friends wanted to talk with me while I was out with Buddy, they would usually call to me from across the street.

On one occasion, my father and I were walking Buddy, with his muzzle on, up 171st Street. From out of nowhere, a cat charged and leaped on Buddy's back. Before we could act, he flipped the cat from off his back and pounced on it with both his paws, breaking its back. We can only surmise that the cat

4

attacked Buddy because she was protecting her kittens, which she must have assumed were threatened by his presence.

My father and I were shaken and remorseful. That episode taught us that we always had to be careful and alert when we walked Buddy. It was rare that anyone other than my father and I, and occasionally my uncle Lewis, ever walked him. But he was an obedient dog.

When Uncle Lewis married, he brought his bride, Muriel, home to live with us until they found their own place. Buddy came to the door and barked loudly when they entered. Uncle Lewis grabbed Buddy by the collar, held him close to Aunt Muriel, and said, "Buddy, this is Muriel. Don't you bother her!" He let Buddy go, and from that point on, Buddy treated Muriel as a regular member of the household.

Like most tenements in the area, our building had mice, and Buddy was great at catching them. If we were out of the house and he caught one, he would put it right in front of the door so that when we entered the house, we usually stepped on it before we saw it. He was always pleased to receive our praise for doing such a good job.

One of Buddy's "mouse-capades" created one of the most hilarious events ever in our household. My cousins Jimmy and Stephen, a.k.a. Buzzy, were at my house. We were all hanging out in the kitchen. On one side of the kitchen, opposite the window that faced an airshaft, was a dumbwaiter that was used to collect the garbage. On the other end of the kitchen, next to the entrance to the hallway, which was on the left, was a chair. To the right of the chair was a wash basin, a sink, and another window that also faced the airshaft. That window had a sill about a foot and a half higher off the floor than the other window.

It was evening, and Mr. Tyson, our super, was "calling the garbage." When the dumbwaiter got to our floor, Mr. Tyson buzzed us to put our garbage on. As my sister opened the dumbwaiter door, a mouse jumped out and onto her shoulder and then onto the floor, where it scurried under the kitchen table. My sister took one step and flew, screaming, eight feet through the air onto the chair at the other end of the kitchen. Meanwhile, Buddy, with lightning speed, pounced under the table to catch the mouse.

My cousins and I were dying with laughter. We could hardly believe what we had seen. My sister could fly! Mr. Tyson was calling up to us to find out what all the screaming was about, and Buddy was proudly displaying his catch. My sister, my cousins, and I always laugh and talk about that day every time we get together. My sister still doesn't believe she flew.

Lesson Learned Along the Way
2. Always be alert and aware of your surroundings.

School Days

Our public schools were neighborhood schools. My elementary school, PS 42, was diagonally across the street from our apartment. It had two schoolyards that ran the length of the school and extended out to Claremont Parkway. I burnished my athletic skills in those yards.

My junior high school, Benjamin Franklin Junior High School, PS 55, was one block south of my apartment and covered the entire square block between St. Paul's Place and East 170th Street and Park and Washington Avenues. It was five stories high, and to us, as young kids, it was physically imposing. It was known as a "tough" school. You could be in physical jeopardy if you couldn't take care of yourself—that is, fight. With both schools so close, we never rode a school bus. Later, when we went on to high school, we used public transportation.

I began kindergarten when I was four. My grandmother would pick me up after class finished. By the time I got to the first grade, I would walk across the street to the school by myself. I remember kindergarten being fun. My mother had already taught me the alphabet and was teaching me how to print and to write in script.

By the time I got to the second grade, the powers that be concluded that I was "troublesome." They transferred me to a special class that they called an "ABC" class. Most of the kids in the class were older than I was, and, as best as I could determine, all had some type of problem, as determined by the teaching corp. They concluded, after observing and testing me, that I knew too much for the second grade, and they promoted me to the third grade.

In those days, we had half grades, such as 3A and 3B, and students could graduate and go on to the next grade in January. To even everything out and have everybody graduate in June, students in the "B" classes that would graduate in January were skipped a half grade so they would eventually graduate in June. But all the students who went through that process had to make up that "skipped term" by having one year of work condensed into a half year.

While I was in elementary school, I started taking piano lessons at home, which my sister had been doing for a few years. She and I were expected to come home, do our homework, and practice our piano lessons so that when our piano teacher, Ms. Woodward, came, we were ready for our lesson. Usually, that's what we did. But every now and then, Jean and I got lazy and didn't practice anywhere near enough. My mother would come home from work and ask if we had practiced our piano lessons, and we would declare that we had. Because my father worked nights at the post office and usually left for work by 4:15 in the afternoon, he was seldom around to hear us practice during the week, so my mother took us at our word.

One week, Jean and I were unusually flagrant in neglecting our practice time, but we lied and told Momma we had practiced diligently. Everything was good until Ms. Woodward came to give us our lessons. By the time each of us got to our tenth note, she could tell we had not practiced a lick. She got so angry with us that she refused to take the money we were supposed to have paid her for our lessons and stormed out of the house. Jean and I knew our asses were grass, and when Momma came home, she was going to be the lawn mower. Ms. Woodward was a woman of great character and her refusing to take her pay was all that needed to be said.

When Momma came home and saw Ms. Woodward's money sitting where she left it, she asked why it was still there. We tried to fudge and soft-pedal and explanation, but that was futile. I don't know which one of us got our spanking first, but that situation never happened again.

Around the time I was in the fifth grade, I began taking tap-dancing lessons at the Mary Bruce School of Dance on 125th Street in Harlem. The studio was above the Baby Grand Nightclub, where the renowned Nipsey Russell usually performed. He was a great comedian, satirist, and performer. It was said that he could recite Chaucer verbatim from memory. Many years later, he performed on game shows, where he displayed his great talent to wider audience. Today, his nightclub performances would only be acceptable on cable or satellite TV because of the language he used. The Baby Grand was one of the top clubs in Harlem, and Mary Bruce School of Dance was the best tap-dancing school in Harlem.

Every year in May and June, Mary Bruce would give two recitals in which all her students would perform. They were always magnificent performances, as anyone who knew her would expect, because she was an outstanding dancer and a perfectionist. In 1947, when I was in the fifth grade, both shows took place at Carnegie Hall, one of our nation's most renowned concert halls.

All the students were asked to sell tickets, and I asked my fifth grade teacher, Ms. Goodman, to buy a couple of tickets. She had a sister who also taught at PS 42, and we distinguished between them as the "skinny" Ms. Goodman, my teacher, and the "fat" Ms. Goodman. When she asked me where the recital would be, and I told her Carnegie Hall, she promptly, deprecatingly, corrected me, saying, "You mean Carnegie Recital Hall!" The Recital Hall was a smaller hall in the same building, and her implication was that it was used by performers of lesser fame and talent and that a black dancing school couldn't be performing at Carnegie Hall.

I insisted that it was "the" Carnegie Hall, and she continued to say I was mistaken. I asked her that if I proved to her it was "the" Carnegie Hall, would she buy a ticket. She boldly pronounced that if it was "the" Carnegie Hall, she would buy ten tickets. I don't know if she attended the recital, but she had to buy the ten tickets to save face. I can't recall ever having a conversation with her about the recital after I collected her money.

The recitals were a great experience. Both recitals were sold out. I can remember walking out onto the stage and being blinded by the floodlights. I could only see some of the audience because of the light reflecting off eyeglasses, primarily from people in the upper balcony. But when we finished our parts, the applause was loud and exhilarating.

I learned to compose myself, that you can be excited without being nervous. Although I did not fully understand what I was instinctively doing at the time, I turned that excitement into positive energy and continued to do so in the years that followed.

Lessons Learned Along the Way.

3. Stand up for yourself.

4. Turn excitement into positive energy.

Junior High School

When I graduated from elementary school, I went to Benjamin Franklin Junior High School. The students who attended came from most of the surrounding neighborhoods, and we all met kids we hadn't known before. I met Albert Webster, who would become one of my closest and lifelong friends. Also, I had my first black teacher, Ms. Saunders, who taught music and conducted the Glee Club.

PS 55 was considered a "rough and tough" school, so you could not be meek and expect to survive. My dad was a man of great character, not easily provoked, very considerate, and always respectful. Although only about five feet, five inches tall and 140 pounds, he didn't take crap from anyone. He taught me to defend myself at an early age and expected me stand up for myself. In the summer before entering PS 55, my friends told me I shouldn't wear my watch to school because someone, probably a gang member, would take it from me. My response was, "Oh yeah, they better be bad because they'll have to fight me for it! If I give it to them, my father will whip my butt, and I don't want that...fighting them will be a lot easier than telling him I 'gave it to some punk!'"

My father's friend Paddy Palmer owned a jewelry store. He taught my father the watch repair trade. My father always gave me a wristwatch, which I usually forgot to remove when playing ball in the schoolyard and usually damaged. I think I enhanced his repair skills because he was always repairing one of my watches. My first troubling encounters in junior high school revolved around my wristwatch.

One boy, Norris, approached me with a threatening demeanor and said, "Nice watch! Can I see it?" I told him, "No." He said, "What if I take it?" When I told him if he thought he could do that to go ahead and try, he backed off, and I went on my way. Shortly thereafter, I was returning to my class from the bathroom when I saw a boy leaning out of a window calling to someone

11

down in the schoolyard. His butt was way up in the air, and I just couldn't refuse the invitation to haul off and smacked him on it. I smacked him so hard that my hand went numb! He recoiled, holding his butt, grimacing, with a look of pain and horror on his face. It was Norris! I walked off, laughing my head off.

He couldn't believe I blasted his ass. Word went out that I was crazy and "you had better be careful if you messed with him."

Another time, one of the school thugs, Clyde, threatened to beat me up after school. I eluded him by using a door that was normally prohibited to students, and by the time he spotted me, I had a good head start. I was too fast for him to run me down. After chasing and failing to catch me, he waited outside my apartment building, daring me to come downstairs so he could "kick my ass." I came out with Buddy on a leash. I gave the command, "Sic him!"

I ran Clyde all the way across the bridge over the Harlem Line tracks on Park Avenue to his doorstep on Brook Avenue four blocks away, where I cornered him. By then, Buddy was foaming at the mouth because his collar was choking him as he tried to overcome my restraint during the chase. Buddy was snarling and barking at Clyde as he tried to melt into the wall next to the doorway. I let Buddy lunge at him repeatedly to where he was inches from Clyde's nose. Clyde was pleading for his life. I told him that the next time he saw me, if he so much as stared at me, I would let Buddy eat him alive.

When I backed away from Clyde, the crowd that had formed scattered. Clyde didn't move. Only his laundry man would know how frightened he was. Buddy and I created another legend, and I was never physically threatened again during junior high school.

Not all my junior high school days were spent defending myself. I grew intellectually and began to expand my knowledge and understanding of our city, country, and world.

The classes of each grade were designated by numbers from 1 to 11. The "1" class was considered the smartest academically, and the "11" class was considered the least capable academically. If you were in classes 9-1 to 9-6, you were on track to attend an academic high school. If you were in classes 9-7 to 9-11, you were on track to pursue a vocational education. Almost all the white students were in the 1, 2, 3, and 4 classes. Few white students were ever in 6 classes and beyond. It was intentional segregation. Students of African descent who were in the 1, 2, 3, and 4 classes were there because their intelligence, academic record, and conduct were so excellent that to be classified any other way would have been an obvious travesty.

Another important factor was that many of the black students in the 1, 2, 3, and 4 classes had parents who were involved in school activities. They understood the game being played in our schools and how it negatively affected their children. These parents had to be on the scene to defend their kids.

I was smart and always achieved good grades. My parents were always checking on what was happening in the school, and they always checked on my sister and me. We had no slack when it came to what was expected of us as students. There were no exceptions. That environment was instrumental in accomplishing one of my first academic achievements: passing the test and being selected to attend Stuyvesant High School.

There were four specialized high schools in New York City in the 1950s, and each required students to pass an entrance exam. The same entrance exam was used for all the schools. Stuyvesant was an all-boys school and was considered one of the finest high schools in the country. The others were the co-ed Bronx High School of Science and Brooklyn Technical High School and the all-girls Hunter High School.

I was one of four students from my junior high school to apply to Stuyvesant High School. The other three boys were kids I grew up with and, to some extent, considered "friends." They were Marvin A., Michael C., and Michael D. I was the only black among the four of us.

Stuyvesant was in Lower Manhattan so we had to take the subway. Once we got on, my three "friends" turned on me. They harassed and taunted me by saying that I was going to fail the test and that they were going to pass and get accepted to Stuyvesant. They didn't stop until we exited the 14th Street station about thirty minutes later and began the five-block walk to the school.

I never doubted that I was smarter than all three of them. Nothing could convince me otherwise. I also knew something they didn't know. About a month earlier, my homeroom teacher had asked me to take some papers pertaining to our test applications to the administrative office. Because they were in a folder and easy to view, I looked at them. The papers contained our IQ scores, and mine exceeded each of theirs.

But it didn't matter because they had infuriated me so much by turning on me that I was determined to excel in that entrance exam. They probably did me a favor because I went into that test room focused like a laser.

At our graduation ceremony, our principal announced the names of my three "friends," stating that one was the recipient of the Math Medal, another the English Medal, and another the Science Medal. One of his concluding comments was "and one of our students was accepted to Stuyvesant High School." He didn't mention my name, but he didn't have to because all the people who mattered to me already knew.

Lessons Learned Along the Way

5. You've got to show up to defend your rights and the rights of loved ones.
6. A positive environment is instrumental for academic achievement.
7. Focus is essential for success.

High School

Stuyvesant High School had two sessions. Juniors and seniors attended the morning session, from 8:05 a.m. to 12:30 p.m. Freshmen and sophomores attended afternoon session, from 12:45 p.m. to 5:25 p.m.

It took time to become accustomed to getting out of school in the dark during the fall and winter. But the greatest disadvantage was if you were a good enough athlete to play on a varsity team as a freshman or sophomore. It was almost impossible to do because the teams practiced and played their games during the afternoon session. If the coach knew an afternoon-session student who was a good player and felt he could help his team, he would try to arrange a "split session" for the student, who would then take some of his courses in the morning session and the remainder during the first part of the afternoon session.

Academically, Stuyvesant was second to none and very competitive. Our worst students would probably have been in the top half of their class if they attended most other high schools. From an academic perspective, there were many intelligent students in the school. But one of the things that became evident to me was that quite a few were common-sense deficient. They were short on "street smarts" and often were thrown off by change. I learned that judging intelligence must be based on more than school grades because when you're in the trenches, relying on someone, that person needs to be mentally tough, adaptable, and able to think on their feet, allowing them to confront and overcome adversity.

Growing up, I was always one of the best athletes in whatever sport I played. I was especially good at baseball and basketball and, to a lesser degree, football. But I rarely had the opportunity to play real football, just touch football in the schoolyard on concrete.

I learned a few other important life lessons in high school because of my participation in sports. One lesson was to be aware of politics.

In my junior year, I worked my way up from the junior varsity basketball team to the varsity team and even played in our division-winning game. It was quite an accomplishment for a five foot seven backcourt man who had to transform his half-court game into that of a full-court playmaker and strong outside shooter.

As a senior, when the varsity tryouts came around, I outplayed every backcourt player in sight. But the star of the team, who was my friend, did not attend the tryouts. He couldn't speak up for me when other team members lobbied the coach for their friends who also happened to be backcourt men. They got their men, and I was relegated to junior varsity, which I decided not to pursue. The two guys who were selected over me warmed the bench all season. Ironically, when the team lost in the league championship game, the two lead lobbyers approached me, saying they "would have won if they had my outside shot on the team."

On many a weekend, we had stickball games that we played for money, either in our neighborhood or in some other part of the Bronx. We usually umpired ourselves and rarely had significant arguments. The most important aspects of the competition were determining the ground rules beforehand when you were the visiting team and deciding who would hold the money that was wagered. In those days, we might play for as much as five dollars a man, but two dollars a man was more common. Nevertheless, that was a lot of money for us back in the late 1940s and early 1950s. The hourly minimum wage increased from forty cents to seventy-five cents in 1949.

The custodian of the money (the "money man") had to be a "bad mamma jammer." He could not be physically intimidated, or you could win the game and still lose. Each team had its own money man. He was usually not a team member but someone's big brother or trusted friend. The team that was leading when the game reached the midpoint got to hold the money. Those games were usually a lot of fun.

When we played softball, the scenario was different regarding the money and the players. This was closer to being professional. All the team members were of the same ilk, but the pitcher had to be a pro, or you got creamed. Because we usually played for more than five dollars a man, the stakes were higher. Our pitcher was Lenny Anderson. We paid him twenty-five dollars a game to pitch for us whether we won or lost. He was a little older than most of us, but he was a pro beyond his years when it came to fast-pitch softball. We seldom lost a game, and I can't recall ever losing a game because of his pitching.

My participation in sports was extensive, and I thought that it might loom large in my future, especially in baseball. But one day in a high school chemistry class, a white classmate of mine (most of the students were white) made an unsolicited and unwelcomed comment to me. It wasn't made out of malice. It was his honest perception. Although I didn't take it kindly, I heard what he said and proceeded to examine his comment. The outcome resulted in the first major decision that I made for myself, which determined the direction of my life.

His statement, which referred to my basketball skills, was, "Wayne, you are a much better than the average player, but you'll never be a pro." Up to that point, I occasionally daydreamed of being a professional athlete, but I had never committed to it. I agreed with him regarding basketball but did not feel that way about baseball. For several days, I examined the point from every position I could perceive.

It was 1953. No African American professional baseball player had made it to the major leagues through the minor league farm system. Every African American ballplayer who made it to the majors was a product of the Negro Leagues. Scouts were not signing black ballplayers who were not proven entities. Certainly, with the exception of Ozzie Virgil, who played sandlot baseball in the Bronx and broke into Major League Baseball with the New York Giants in 1956, scouts weren't taking a chance on those of us playing in the sandlot leagues. If I was going to make it to the major leagues, I would have to concentrate my efforts to succeed with such intensity that my chance of graduating from college would be minimal. On top of that, the final decisions on my progress would never be in my control. My decision was that I would continue to enjoy and participate in baseball and basketball, but my job would be to get a college education.

The classmate that started me on that decisionmaking journey was Herbert Brand. We graduated a year later in 1954 and went our separate ways. Our paths crossed twice after that. The first time was five years later, when we both were selected to attend the US Navy Officer Candidate School and entered class 45. I was in JULIETT Company, and he was in MIKE Company, and we met, after several weeks, by chance. The second time we encountered each other was in 1962, when I was on "temporary additional duty" as the meteorological officer for the advanced aviation base at Souda Bay, Crete in the Mediterranean Sea. He was on a plane that was passing through, and we met shortly before the Cuban Missile Crisis began.

Years later, in a discussion about education with my mother, she was in disbelief when I related to her that I considered college a "job," and I attended as a necessary means to an end to secure a chance for a better life for myself, not because I was enthralled with education. The first time I attended school on my own volition for the primary purpose of obtaining an education was when I went to Baruch College, City University of New York, for six years at night to attain my MBA in international business.

Lessons Learned Along the Way
8. Evaluate intelligence on more than school grades.
9. Be aware of politics going on behind your back.
10. Always determine the ground rules in advance.
11. Interpret unsolicited advice thoughtfully, and evaluate the motives of the advice giver.

College

One thing I realized I could have done better in high school was to put in an hour more of studying each day. It probably would have resulted in my overall academic average being three to four points higher, which would have placed me in the top third of my high school class instead of the middle third. It cost me a few full scholarships. The partial ones I was offered, I determined, were not worth the financial strain they would have placed on my parents. So I went to the "poor people's Harvard," City College of the College of the City of New York (CCNY).

Up to that time, the five years I spent in CCNY, now the City College of the City University of New York, were the five toughest years of my life. I started out in the School of Engineering. By the end of my second year, I was convinced that I didn't want to become a mechanical engineer. So I transferred into the School of Arts and Science. After two semesters, I discovered my love and inherent interest in meteorology, which I decided to make my major.

The inherent interest came from my early love of airplanes and flying that was nurtured by my uncle Lewis, who became a master flight mechanic as a member of the Tuskegee Airmen. He was so good that the command would deny his request for transfers overseas because he was needed to train fledgling mechanics. Uncle Lewis would send me a copy of all the latest aircraft identification books of that World War II era. I couldn't draw a lick, but I became an expert at aircraft identification and could draw flawless front, side, and bottom views of every aircraft in the books. I maintained that identification skill throughout my naval career and to this day.

Meteorology fit me like an expensive hand-tailored suit. I was also fortunate that there were only ten or eleven meteorology majors, so our advanced classes were small. Our instruction was excellent, and our major instructors were military veterans or reservists who had experience in the field. During that time, I met one of my lifelong friends, Richard Crisci, who had a career in the US Weather Bureau, which was incorporated into the National Oceanic and Atmospheric Administration as the National Weather Service.

During that time, in 1957, I also met Mowbrey McKinley, who would become my daughter's godmother seventeen year later. Her first husband, Benjamin Frowner, and his twin brother, Byron, also attended Stuyvesant High School. They would also attend CCNY, which is where Benjamin met Mowbrey.

I briefly encountered Colin Powell at CCNY. He was in the Army Reserve Officers' Training Corp (ROTC) and went on to have an outstanding military career, chair the Joint Chiefs of Staff, and become secretary of state. Our paths didn't cross much, and I would not say we knew each other, but we had a "nodding acquaintance."

I knew the Ronald Brooks whom he met while in the ROTC and who became his lifelong friend and mentor, when I was in my early teens. I also came to know Colin Powell's cousin, Bruce Llewellyn, later in my communications career. Bruce was a lawyer and became a successful businessman. He also sponsored me to become a member of "The One Hundred Black Men," an influential group of prominent businessmen and professionals. (One Hundred Black Men Inc. began in New York City as an organization of like-minded business, political, and community leaders convened to capitalize on the collective power of community to address issues of concern, inequities, and to empower African Americans to be agents for change in their own communities.)

I am proud of Colin Powell's achievements. They are especially gratifying because he, too, is a native of the South Bronx and born of West Indian parents. We are products of parents who managed their lives based on a heritage of high moral character, dedication to maximizing opportunity for their family, and a commitment to excellence.

I found CCNY to be tough and demanding primarily because no one held your hand and walked you through the learning process. You were lectured and told what you had to do. Demonstrations and guidance were not a given. You had to find a way to get it done and done correctly. To be successful, you had to learn how to learn. Getting a break on a grade was rare.

One of the few breaks I received was from my chemistry teacher, Mr. Scharf, during my freshman year. I was good in chemistry when I was in high school, but that subject in CCNY was a nightmare. I struggled to get a passing grade. Late one morning, a day or so after I took my final exams, I was taking the subway to school to find out my grades for the semester. As I entered the D train, I saw Mr. Scharf, sat down next to him, and asked him how I did on the exam. It was convenient because he was on the way to CCNY to post the grades. He showed me how he arrived at our grades, considering the fact that no student in my class passed his final exam. I had the second-highest grade on the test, a paltry 36.

Because he marked the test on a curve, I was given a D and was thrilled to get it. When my father saw my D, he asked why I did so poorly. I told him my final exam grade was the second-highest grade in the class. He told me, "I don't care what someone else did. I am only concerned about you." I was not expected to perform in relation to someone else. I was expected to achieve my maximum capability.

In my next-to-last year at CCNY, I was required to take a language. I chose French. It was the only class I had on Thursdays, and I did not have any Friday classes. I decided to have dental work one Thursday morning at 11:00 a.m. before I went to French class at 2:00 that afternoon, even though I knew we had an exam that day. I didn't know the dental work would require Novocain because I had never had dental work that required a painkiller before. I took it without knowing what effect it might have on me.

Although my mouth was a little numb, I felt fine after the dentist gave me an inlaid filling, and I went to school feeling capable of taking my French exam. But just before the test began, the Novocain began to wear off, and the

21

pain and soreness in my mouth became so intense that I couldn't concentrate and failed the test. Although I passed the final, I didn't achieve a high enough grade to average a C.

My instructor was new to CCNY and told me that she had to give me a D because the department head warned her that she was being too generous with her grading and needed to be tougher. If I had gotten a 68 average, one point higher, she could have given me a C. The result, the real damage, was that I lost my matriculated status and had to pay for my last year of school. (Until the 1990s, CCNY was free to students who qualified via their high school grades.)

I felt bad about becoming a nonmatriculated student and thought it was unfair to burden my parents with the tuition after all the sacrifices they had made to get me through college. I never even considered whether they could pay the tuition for me to complete college. I had been saving a little money from the various jobs I had been working while in college, for a vacation to Paris. I used those funds instead to pay for my last two college semesters.

The courses I took the last two semesters, except for physical education, were all meteorology courses, in which I performed well, attaining Bs and As.

Lessons Learned Along the Way
12. Study an extra hour a day. It can improve your class standing and enhance your knowledge base.
13. You must learn *how* to learn.
14. Perform at *your* maximum capability, not in relation to your peers.
15. Be careful how, when, and why you use medication.

Graduation picture from City College of New York, June 17, 1959.

Launching My Career

During my last year in college, I met recruiters from the US Air Force and the US Navy, both of which needed people for their meteorological skills. The other major entity that needed my skills was the US Weather Bureau. There were few private meteorological companies. A few airlines had meteorology departments, but airlines were risky because whenever the industry slumped, meteorologists were the first to be laid off because airlines could always use the Weather Bureau.

After World War II, there was a universal draft. Most people who volunteered for the armed forces selected the navy or the air force, but we did not have an all-volunteer military. All males, upon turning eighteen, were required to register for the draft. I always knew that I would be subjected to the draft when I graduated college, and there was no doubt in my mind that I was officer material. Early in my college career, it became my objective to fulfill my military obligation as an officer. So I was receptive to the recruiters, who were invited to meet and brief us about military opportunities.

Even though I came from a long line of seafarers on my mother's side, I was partial to the air force because of my uncle's service as a Tuskegee Airman and the examples of black officers attaining the highest ranks in that branch of the service. My perception of the navy was tainted by its history of limited opportunities for black sailors, but I chose to pursue acceptance into the US Navy Officer Candidate School (OCS) because the navy officer who recruited me made it clear that the "navy wanted me." It was one of the best and most important decisions of my life. I was proud, as were my family and friends, when I was accepted into and later graduated from OCS.

Until then, City College had been the greatest challenge I had ever faced. When I entered OCS, I discovered what a real challenge was! When I was notified of my acceptance, I had been working for three weeks in my first career job as meteorologist for the US Weather Bureau in the New York City office. When I applied for the job and was interviewed by the assistant meteorologist in charge, Charlie Knudsen, a US Naval Reserve lieutenant commander, I informed him that I had applied for OCS. He said to me, "You know only 10 percent of those who apply for OCS are accepted?" I told him, "I expect to be in that 10 percent!"

I was the first meteorology graduate to join the New York City office in three years. During the three weeks before my notification, I made rapid progress in learning my forecasting duties. Charlie was impressed, so much so that he had scheduled me to start working solo shifts beginning my fourth week. When I showed him the OCS letter of acceptance, he smacked the letter, mildly cursed, and congratulated me. He then mapped out a plan for the four weeks before I reported to OCS in Newport, Rhode Island.

The plan allowed me to work in every job in the office, including radar meteorology, research, receptionist, and forecaster. I was exposed to almost all aspects of running a meteorological office. The most significant event during that period was my stint as the radar meteorologist. In 1959, radar was "the new thing" in weather forecasting

While scanning the radar, I observed a "hook" on the scope, a couple hundred miles east of Baltimore, Maryland. (A funnel cloud is a tornado when it touches the ground or a waterspout when it touches the water surface. On the early radars, which were not designed for weather observation, a funnel cloud appeared as a hook.) I marked the coordinates and showed the duty meteorologist my observation. Because he had been trained in radar meteorology and I had not, he could not fathom that I knew what I observed. I asked him, "Isn't a 'hook' representative of a funnel cloud?" He replied in the affirmative, but he still couldn't get up enough courage to take the chance of relying on my observation, so he would not send out the report on the teletype. When the next observations came in, we saw an observation from a ship at sea that reported the funnel cloud I had observed on the radar. The duty meteorologist saw the report and apologized for his lack of confidence in my report. He was amazed at my ability to interpret what I saw when it took him many days of training to accomplish the skill.

Lesson Learned Along the Way
16. Think ahead. Visualize your future.

MY NAVY YEARS

On Monday, July 20, 1959, I was sworn in to the US Navy Reserve at the recruiting headquarters on Broadway in Lower Manhattan. On July 27, my parents saw me off at Grand Central Terminal as I boarded the New York, New Haven, and Hartford Railroad train bound for Providence, Rhode Island, where I would catch a bus to the navy base at Newport.

My dad, who was proud of me, said little. He wished me well but gave no hugs. My mom was happy that I wasn't heading to the southern US, where she would fear for my safety. If I went to the south, she foresaw a white person calling me a "nigger" and me, with my temper, reacting aggressively and being lynched, all of which was not far-fetched. She was happy and proud of my accomplishment but sad that I was leaving home.

I was full of emotions, some of which I had never experienced. I was proud to go to OCS. It was the first time I was leaving home. When the train left the station, I was taken aback when I felt homesickness for the first time. I thought OCS would be the beginning of an adventure, but I knew it was going to be a major challenge.

The navy was not viewed as the place to be for blacks. Its World War II reputation was still the vision that most African Americans perceived. In addition, I sensed my entire community was counting on me to succeed, an additional burden. That burden was not relieved when I reported to the school and saw that among the 1,050 officer candidates in my class, only two, George Washington King and I, were of African descent. George and I were on the same train from New York, took the same bus to Newport, and were ordered to line up in formation when we disembarked. Both of us ended up in Juliett Company, section 4 of class 45. The biggest challenge of my life was about to begin.

Officer Candidate School

The barracks we would occupy at OCS were constructed of wood, and we were told that in a fire, they could be engulfed in three minutes. That was about twice as long as it would take my apartment building home to go up in smoke, so I wasn't upset to learn that. I had lived under that kind of life-threatening pressure my entire life.

The classrooms were always hot in the summer and always cold in the winter. You were instructed that if you felt like you were going to doze during a lecture or audiovisual session, you should get up and stand in the back of the room. Falling asleep in class could get you in deep trouble.

Many officer candidates were accustomed to getting a great deal of sleep, but because we had study hall every weeknight—usually from 7:00 p.m. to 10:00 p.m., unless you were granted "late lights," which would allow you to study until 11:00 p.m.—or you might have to stand a watch from 8:00 p.m. to 8:00 a.m., you sleep time could be short. The barracks and classrooms were not air conditioned. We normally had only three hours a night to study what amounted to about ten hours of homework. Fortunately for me, I functioned well on five and a half hours of sleep, so I took advantage of late lights almost every night.

We were the maintenance crew for the old barracks. One of our first assignments was to clean the entire barracks, including mopping, scraping, and waxing floors and making the place livable. Because each incoming class lived in different barracks, that was a means of keeping them in tip-top condition. During that first week, we also got fitted for our dress uniforms and received our work uniforms, received our shots, and were told about what was expected of us and what was to come.

On Saturday morning, we could attend our various religious services, and by 11:00, we would be in formation marching to the "grinder," the field on which the entire class formed up, marched, and were addressed by our commandant and other officers. After that, if we did not have any demerits to march off, we would be on our way to "liberty," the naval term for time off.

Our first liberty was supposed to take place on our second weekend. But because our uniforms were not ready, we were not allowed to go "ashore"—that is, leave the base. So we participated in various activities on the base, such as playing basketball. During that second weekend, I got my first naval nickname.

Some of my classmates and I were playing basketball. One player was Jonesy, who was from Alabama and spoke with a distinct southern accent. He was our company commander but later got "rolled back" to the next class because of his poor grades. If he hadn't been the company commander, he might have been sent to the fleet as an enlisted man, but he got another chance. He started to talk and joke about what he would do when he got liberty. He asked me what my plan was. I told him I was going to the "Big Apple." He said, "What the hell is the 'Big Apple'?" I chided him and told him it was a nickname for New York City. From then on, Jonesy always referred to me as "Big Apple." I was pleased that the nickname didn't become widespread.

After dinner, we had an hour or so before study hall to relax, which is a poor description of how we used that time. We would shine our shoes, which became a therapeutic exercise for me, and prepare our uniforms for the next day. We might have a locker inspection. If your locker wasn't neat and well organized, you would receive a demerit, which you would have to march off on the grinder, an hour for each one, before you went on liberty. If you had too many, you would not get liberty. I never knew of anyone being that bad who remained in OCS.

Most of my classmates were terrified of locker inspections. For me, they were a piece of cake. Because of my upbringing, my locker was always ready for inspection. My room, drawers, and closets at home were always in order, so keeping that little locker at OCS straight was a breeze. But your classmates could torpedo you if you weren't careful.

The only time I ever got a demerit was for a "loose bunk," and I could not believe it! My mother taught me to make a bed before I went to Bronx House Camp when I was eight. No way could my bedding have been loose! My classmate, Jack Simon, whose bunk was above me, got a similar demerit. He was a really nice guy, but he was sloppy. He was pissin' and moanin' about inspections and said when he came back to the barrack after his watch, before he left, he sat on my bunk. I chewed him out, and we marched on the grinder together the following Saturday, losing three hours of much-needed liberty.

There was not any significant racial or ethnic diversity in OCS, certainly not in class 45, but there was plenty of geographical diversity. Officer candidates came from all over the country. We had guys who had never seen a body of water larger than a river or a lake. Many had never visited a large city, and many had never seen an ocean. Social adaptation and conformity were necessary to survive and succeed in OCS and in their future naval careers. It was my experience that candidates from the south had to make the biggest adjustments.

Officer candidates Jack Simon and Wayne Sobers on their first liberty, August 1959.

In 1959, the south was still segregated, and the battle for our civil rights, especially in that region, was building momentum but was not near at hand. There were many white people, not only white southerners, who did not appreciate black folks being among them as equals. Officer Candidate School, for many in my platoon, was a brand-new experience.

One September day in 1959, it got chilly, and many of my classmates were not dressed for the abrupt change in temperature. Eugene Rairden, a Virginian, about six feet five with a pale complexion, was sitting in the row in front of me and one seat over in class, next to the window, which was open about four inches. I happened to look over at him and noticed that he was shivering, so I reached over and closed the window. Rairden turned around and looked at me in disbelief. Later in the day he asked me, "Sobers, why did you close the window?" I said, "I looked over and saw you shivering and about to turn blue. It occurred to me that if the window was closed, you wouldn't be quite as cold. So, I closed it."

I don't recall him ever saying thank you. We didn't speak much after that. But in November, at the end of our commissioning ceremony, many OCS graduates, now commissioned naval officers, were congregating with their families and friends in the parking lot preparing to depart. Suddenly, I saw Rairden leading an air force lieutenant colonel by the arm walking toward me. The air force officer was his father, to whom he wanted to introduce me. I saluted him. He congratulated me and wished me well. I assumed it was Rairden's way of telling me thanks and acknowledging that his regard for black officers, and maybe black people in general, had undergone a positive change.

And then there was Jonesy. He brought to light for me another perspective, that of a white American's personal conflicts in trying to reconcile his prejudicial beliefs.

We were on liberty for the weekend and headed to the Mooring, a bar in downtown Newport. Upon entering, I saw Jonesy sitting at the far end of the bar with his head in his hands and a drink in front of him. I gravitated over to him and asked, "How you doing?" He said, "Sit down, Big Apple," patting the seat to his right. "I need to talk with you." I sat down.

He began the conversation by saying, "I got a problem." He told me that before he arrived at OCS, he only knew and experienced life in an environment that was based on racial segregation. He never encountered or associated with black people on an equal level. But since he became an officer candidate and came to know "King George" (George Washington King's nickname) and me, he realized that, aside from our skin color, there wasn't any real differences between us. He said, "When I go home, I'm going to want to meet an interact with black people like you and King George, and I can't do that in Alabama."

He was troubled, and I couldn't help him, and I told him so. I told him that I respected his revelation and understood he was in a difficult and conflicting situation. But it was a situation he would have to resolve himself. I don't know if he ever found the solution he was looking for. I didn't encounter him after he got rolled back.

Midway through our sixteen weeks of classes, I decided I would not travel back home when on weekend liberty until I completed and graduated from OCS. I thought those final eight weeks would be tougher to take than they turned out to be, the reason being that I had met Audrey Britton several months before I graduated from CCNY and entered OCS. When I came home, my primary purpose was to see her and be with her. I was going to miss her over those next eight weeks, but I knew I had to increase my focus to succeed, graduate, and get commissioned as an ensign in the US Navy.

Audrey Lorraine (Britton) Sobers

I met Audrey at a party hosted by my neighbor and friend, Dorothy Smith, who lived two houses away. Audrey knew who I was, but I was unaware of her. She knew me as being a prominent member of the Aristons (formerly St. Paul's Episcopal Church) basketball team, whose games she would occasionally attend. Many of my teammates lived or hung out in her Morrisania neighborhood.

She was attractive, quiet, unassuming, and sweet. When she walked into Dotty's apartment, I was so stricken by her that I almost stopped dancing with my partner in the middle of the record that was playing. Audrey was wearing a beautiful white dress with what I thought were bright red polka dots. When I later recounted to her what pattern I thought I had seen on her dress, she said they were not red polka dots but red flowers. My incorrect impression confirmed how deeply I was struck when I first saw her.

For the remainder of that evening, I was oblivious to everyone and everything except Audrey. I asked if she would go on a date with me, and she consented. She and her parents had moved to the Hunts Point section of the Bronx in advance of the impending housing project that was slated to replace ten square blocks of her neighborhood. She gave me her telephone number. I had nothing to write it on, but I remembered it for years.

Audrey Lorraine (Britton) Sobers, 1960

Commissioning was upon me. I survived the final eight weeks without visiting the Big Apple to see Audrey. As soon as I confirmed that I had passed all my classes and would be commissioned an ensign, I began growing my mustache back, which I had to remove when I entered OCS. We had a commissioning ball that Audrey attended. My parents, sister, nephew, and brother-in-law all attended my commissioning ceremony on November 19, 1959.

It was a great day! George Washington King and I gave each other a nod of congratulations. After all, we were the only black OCS candidates in a class that started with 1,050 candidates. Approximately 20 percent of candidates either flunked out or were rolled back. The final tally for my class was 713 graduates, which translated to a 32 percent attrition rate. George and I deserved to give each other more than a nod of congratulations, but we had to maintain our cool until we had our privacy.

Many of our fellow officer candidates had never interacted with people of African descent, so their experiences with us, for many of them, was life altering and ultimately, I believe, made them better naval officers. People like George and me carried the flags of our communities, not just throughout OCS, but throughout our naval careers. We both had a lot to be proud of, and the nod we gave each other acknowledged that.

During the second half of the class, each candidate submitted a request for duty station or area assignments following their commissioning. There was one other meteorologist in my class. He requested assignment in the continental US, and I requested assignment in the Caribbean. Neither of us received our choices. He was assigned to Roosevelt Roads Naval Station in Puerto Rico, and I was assigned to the US Naval Weather Facility at the Naval Air Station in Quonset Point, Rhode Island, which was across the bay from OCS. One of my first navy lessons? You were assigned where the navy needed you. If you got your choice, you lucked out.

I got great experience, learned a great deal, and performed well at the Naval Weather Facility. It also provided Audrey and me ample opportunity to develop a wonderful, fulfilling, and loving relationship. There was no doubt marriage was in our future. The one issue was that she had had ulcerative colitis since she was twelve years old. It never affected my desire to marry her. I wanted to spend my life with her, and we would learn to cope with her illness together for the rest of our lives. She was my angel, and I loved her without any reservations.

Ensign Waynett A. Sobers Jr., November 1959

Naval Air Station Quonset Point

After a week or so of military leave, I reported to my first duty station, the Fleet Weather Facility on Quonset Point. It was on Naval Air Station Quonset Point, the home base for several antisubmarine squadrons and the USS Essex.

The USS Essex had served in World War II with distinction and had the nickname "Fightin'est Ship in the Fleet." It was the first of the twenty-four Essex-class aircraft carriers built during the war. It was decommissioned in 1947, modernized and recommissioned in 1951 as an attack carrier, and reclassified as an antisubmarine aircraft carrier in 1960. I met William M. McGhee, another African American officer, when he was assigned to the USS Essex upon his completion of OCS. We would later reconnect in Italy, where we would serve and become lifelong friends.

I was, to my knowledge, the only African American officer assigned to the air station. I had an African American petty officer, first class, among my aerographer mates named "Smitty," who was the senior enlisted man in the unit. He was a competent leader with a good sense of humor. Each summer, he would get temporary additional duty to Antarctica for several months where it was winter. We referred to it as "winter over."

It was an assignment to which I occasionally gave thought, but not much. I did not think I would appreciate the isolation and confinement that the duty dictated. It was not yet the age of satellite communications, TV, and the like. You had to tolerate the men you would work with and appreciate the work you had to perform or the environment, which I imagined could become unpleasant. My motivation to consider it was the thought of how much money I could save because my basic subsistence down there would be minimal, and there wasn't anything worthwhile to spend money on.

The officers I served with at the Fleet Weather Facility were fine people. We got along well, and they gave me a good and unselfish orientation.

They had worked out a duty schedule that generated blocks of free time—that is, twelve-hour days and thirteen-hour nights with rotating weekends. When the new commanding officer, Commander James Shoemaker, assumed command, that schedule ended.

My duties were many. We conducted all the weather briefings for the departing flight operations at Naval Air Station Quonset Point. We briefed President Eisenhower's flight crew every morning when he vacationed in the area. His plane, a Lockheed Constellation, was named the Columbine. (During the Eisenhower presidency, the call sign "Air Force One" was created for the president's plane.) Each day, we provided the weather forecast, including sea conditions, for the Narragansett operating area, which was an area of about 150 square miles in the Atlantic Ocean, south of Cape Cod, Massachusetts, where training exercises were frequently conducted; the local weather forecast for the Naval Air Station Quonset Point and Naval Station Newport area; and flight forecasts between Quonset Point and Argentia, Newfoundland. In addition, we briefed the navy's Blue Angels and the air force's Thunderbirds when they performed in the area, and we were third in line for hurricane forecasting on the East Coast.

There were three major naval facilities (Naval Air Station Quonset Point, Naval Station Newport, and Davisville Naval Construction Battalion Center) and US Coast Guard stations in and around Narragansett Bay, Rhode Island, so our duties and services were critical.

A couple of events stand out from my time at the Fleet Weather Facility.

One afternoon in February or March 1960, while on duty, I received a telephone call from a retired admiral (let's call him Admiral Smith). He prefaced his request by stating that he knew what he was about to ask might be difficult to fulfill. His request was for me to help him choose one of two Saturdays in July for him to give a garden party. I frowned, grabbed my head, asked him for his telephone number, and told him I would do my best to assist him. I promised to get back to him in few days with an answer.

I had no idea how I might tackle this request. The task was nearly impossible because there were no long-term forecasting tools capable of predicting weather events that far in advance. The only tools I could use were our climatological records. I put one of my crew to work going through the base's and area's records. We found that of the dates requested, the earlier date had rain one more time than the later date. I called the admiral and suggested that "if I were giving the party, I would choose the later date." He thanked me, and I hung up, believing that was the end of it.

Shortly after, Commander Shoemaker came on board as the commanding officer. He ran a tighter ship than his predecessor and always kept his finger on the pulse of the base and our facility. The commander was focused on being promoted to the rank of captain and would not tolerate anything that might derail that objective. When he walked toward me one day that July with a quizzical look on his face, I took notice. He asked me if I was familiar with an Admiral Smith. I couldn't recall who it was until Shoemaker told me that the admiral mentioned it was about a "forecast I gave him." It all came back to me, and I remembered that his party should have taken place by then. Commander Shoemaker said, "He's on the phone." I answered the phone with artificial confidence. "Good day, Admiral Smith!"

He thanked me for assisting him and told me what a great success his party was. He ended the conversation by congratulating me on my skill and professionalism. All the while, Commander Shoemaker stood behind me trying to ascertain why this admiral had requested to speak with this (lowly) ensign. The garden party had taken place the previous Saturday, a magnificent day. The Saturday before that (the earlier date), it had rained.

I explained to Commander Shoemaker what had prompted the admiral's call. I told the commander that I relied on climatology to make my forecast, but I didn't tell him how I used it. Why blur my image? My stock, in the commander's view, went up.

The second major event was when a "green card" pilot, an air force colonel, looked down on my rank and disrespected my ability and, possibly, my race. Whichever it was, his actions nearly cost him and his crew their lives.

Pilots who have green cards are highly qualified and can approve or sign their own flight plans, or DD175s. They did not need the duty meteorologist or the duty operations officer to approve them. Nevertheless, those pilots would always go to the weather office and request flight forecasts for their proposed trips.

This particular winter day was one of the worst weather days I had experienced. The entire northeastern US was one unstable low-pressure system, full of intense thunderstorms and heavy to severe icing. We had already had one cargo plane barely make it over the seawall with its two starboard engines feathered (propellers not rotating) and another cargo plane with one of its two port engines feathered. Each had experienced heavy turbulence and severe icing.

The air force colonel had landed at Quonset earlier and filed a flight plan to fly to an airbase in the Midwest. I briefed the colonel and informed him that the icing conditions were severe. He argued that he "could fly above the icing." But I pointed out that his flight plan indicated that he wouldn't reach the altitude where he would be above the severe icing until he was over Buffalo, New York. That meant he would be climbing in severe icing for close to an hour after takeoff. I urged him not to go, but he dismissed my advice and went anyway. The operations officer called me and asked me what I had advised the colonel to do. The DD175 that I filled out was a "horror story," and I told the operations officer to look at it again and tell me if he ever saw one more terrifying. He couldn't believe the air force colonel was going to attempt the flight.

In less than forty-five minutes, the tower alerted us to an impending emergency. The colonel's plane was inbound and partially crippled. It barely made the runway on two engines. The colonel came storming into operations, came up to my office, and called me everything but a child of God. He threatened to "write me up." I was furious, but I maintained my cool. When he finished his rant, I told him to "go back down and examine the DD175 that you signed and approved. If you do, I doubt you'll be man enough to come back to this office an apologize to me." He went down to operations and pulled the DD175. The operations officer told me he looked at it and then tossed it and stormed out.

My duty at the Fleet Weather Facility provided me with many firsts that were valuable to me as a meteorologist, as a naval officer, and as a man. Up until my assignment to the weather facility, I had never flown in a plane. Because I knew so much about airplanes from my uncle Lewis, I regarded that deficiency as a flaw in my training that had to be rectified.

As a meteorologist with flight forecasting responsibility, I worked with many pilots. My knowledge of the technical capability of their aircraft enhanced my ability to provide them superior flight forecasts. But to fully empathize with pilots and the situations they encountered, I needed flight time so I could see the dynamics of the atmosphere the way they felt and viewed them. I let every pilot assigned to the Naval Air Station know that I wanted to fly with them whenever possible.

Commander Perry, a likable, grey-haired veteran US Coast Guard aviator, took me up on my first flight in an Albatross, a twin-engine seaplane whose primary mission was search-and-rescue operations. It normally flew low and slow. When it was climbing to its operating altitude, it was so slow that someone like me, unaccustomed to the aircraft's characteristics, had to look out the window to make sure we were flying. I got to sit in the copilot's seat and took in every tidbit of information the commander shared with me while absorbing all that my eyes could see.

After that, I took many familiarization flights down the East Coast to Washington, DC, and north to Naval Air Station Brunswick in Maine. At Naval Air Station Brunswick, I met Lieutenant Benjamin Thurman Hacker, an African American naval aviation observer assigned to a patrol squadron based there. We had a good time sharing our life experiences. Ben would become the first naval flight officer to achieve Flag rank in the US Navy and the first naval flight officer to lead Commander Fleet Air Mediterranean (COMFAIRMED) in Naples, Italy, which would become my next duty station. He had a distinguished naval career, had ten commands, and had a significant business career.

The second part of my mission was to obtain flight time in jet aircraft. But that required getting qualified in the ejection seat, and while I was at it, I also got "checked out" in the night vision trainer. The latter was enlightening, and the training helped me with my efforts to upgrade my crew's observational techniques. I was ready to fly on a rocket.

There was a pilot assigned to the Naval Air Station whom I frequently briefed when he flew, which mostly was for maintaining his flight status. I approached him and asked if he would let me fly in the back seat of his two-seat trainer the next time he took it up. He said he would.

On the day of our training flight, the eastern US was under a strong high-pressure weather system. The weather was perfect. The sky was "CAVU" (clear and visibility unlimited). When we took off and the air conditioning was turned on, I was blasted by ice crystals. The pilot warned me not to touch the top of the instrument panel, which was black and became hot in the sunlight. With no clouds in the sky, sitting under a thick plexiglass canopy, the cockpit was oven-like, so the air conditioning was necessary.

I had never ever seen such a spectacular view in my life! We were cruising 35,000 feet above New York City. I could see the southern tip of New Jersey, Cape May, approximately 160 miles south. The Atlantic Ocean glistened. Montauk Point, Long Island, 125 miles to the east, and Block Island further east yet, were also in view.

From a meteorological perspective, I would have gained more from the flight if the weather had been cloudy with various cloud layers and if there had been some turbulence. After all, clouds are indicative of the atmosphere's dynamic state, and that's what meteorology is all about. I had many more familiarization flights, all of which supplemented my knowledge base and enhanced my flight forecasting skills. But I would not have traded that day for anything.

About four months after I reported to the Fleet Weather Facility, I began an effort to get an assignment in Europe, preferably in Spain, where I might have a chance to participate in the running of the bulls in Pamplona. So even though I anticipated the request would be denied (it was), I believed the request would put me on the record at the Bureau of Personnel as desiring such an assignment. I don't know if it did or not, but in January 1961, when I submitted a request for a transfer to the Naval Station Rota in Spain, the bureau told me that there "was no vacant meteorological billets." But the director of the US Naval Weather Service recommended I be "ordered to the Staff, Commander Fleet Air Mediterranean, (Naples, Italy) as relief for LCDR [Lieutenant Commander] R. M. Roland, whose rotation date is July 1961."

It was a minor coup for an ensign to get such a prime duty assignment after only seventeen months as an officer. After I reported there, I discovered that a few behind-the-scenes factors had worked in my favor. The officer I was replacing was out of favor with the COMFAIRMED command. It wasn't about his work. It was personal. He had a local Italian girlfriend with whom he lived.

In Naples, the various naval commands had a "female spy" complex. They were paranoid and believed that any officer who was in an intimate relationship with an Italian woman would inevitably share secret information with her, which the woman would then share with the "enemy." An officer in that situation could not hold a billet that required a top-secret clearance.

The COMFAIRMED chief of staff, a captain who wanted to be promoted to admiral, did not like Roland's lifestyle. He detested the way Roland wore his hat, tilted to the left side, and he probably didn't like Roland's mustache either, and he had refused to approve Roland's request for an extension.

Lessons Learned Along the Way

17. Your ego can destroy you. Keep it in check.

18. Try to recognize your deficiencies. Correct them if possible.

Naples, Italy

Before receiving my notification of transfer to COMFAIRMED, several fellow officers were riding me about the likelihood of its approval. Many of them were members of VAW-24, an early-warning squadron that deployed with various aircraft carriers as part of its advanced air defense. One of the officers was Lieutenant John Everett Fox, a pilot whose suite was on the other side of the bathroom we shared.

After a lot of banter between us and others in VAW-24, we made a bet. If my transfer request was approved, I would be assigned to either the base at Rota, Spain, or the base at Naples, Italy. The USS Forrestal, on which their squadron deployed as part of the Sixth Fleet in the Mediterranean Sea, would "call" on both ports. If I got transferred to one of those locations, when their ship arrived, I would notify them, and they would "party" me. If my request was not approved, when they returned from their deployment, I would "party" them.

During the seventeen months I was stationed in Rhode Island, there was no question that I wanted to marry Audrey and that she wanted to marry me. She knew about my request for a transfer to Europe, and I told her if my going there without her meant I would lose her, I would marry her on the spot. But I thought I needed to "sow a few more wild oats" before I took that step.

She, too, was not ready to take that leap. Nevertheless, she professed her love for me and her desire for us to marry. She also wanted to continue her education. I knew that when we tied the knot, she would be fully committed to our life together.

Audrey was an only child, and after we married and she joined me in Italy, she told me that she had never spent a night alone in her life, at home or anyplace else.

On May 8, 1961, I reported to McGuire Air Force Base in Trenton, New Jersey, for transportation to Naples via Frankfurt, Germany. It was my first flight on a Pan Am Boeing 707, which would fly nonstop to Rhein-Main Airport in Frankfurt. The flight arrived there early the next morning, and because I sleep poorly on all forms of transportation and feared that if I slept during the day I would not be able to sleep that night, I stayed up and staggered through the day until nightfall. That allowed me to get a good night's sleep and be prepared for my flight to Rome the following day.

That following day, I flew on an Alitalia DC9 to Rome. Because I had several hours before my evening Alitalia flight to Naples, I went into Rome and viewed several sites, the most impressive of which was the Colosseum. I was in awe when I toured it. To walk into a 2,000-year-old building with such a history was amazing. As I returned to the airport to catch my flight to Naples, I thought that Italy was going to be good for me.

Naval Air Facility Naples shares runways with Naples Airport. The evening of May 11, 1961, I reported for duty in Naples via the naval air facility. The next morning, I reported aboard at COMFAIRMED on Via Manzoni, just north of the city's heart.

Duty at COMFAIRMED would become one of the most interesting, challenging, educational, self-fulfilling, and gratifying times of my life. One of my class 45 OCS classmates, whom I hardly knew, was on the staff. Upon my arrival, I was greeted and ushered around by the personnel officer, Lieutenant Patricia (Pat) Donovan. My department head was a lieutenant commander who was the atomic, biological, and chemical warfare officer. During my assignment at COMFAIRMED, I interacted with him infrequently because I was a meteorological officer at Naval Air Facility Naples when I was not performing other staff functions.

Lieutenant (junior grade) Wayne Sobers conducting a flight weather briefing at Naval Air Facility Naples, Italy, 1961

Lieutenant (junior grade) Wayne Sobers at Naval Air Facility Naples, Italy, circa 1961–62

My primary COMFAIRMED staff function was temporary additional duty aboard the USS Alameda County and the USS Tallahatchie County. The Alameda County was an old converted landing ship tank that had seen service in World War II in the Atlantic and Pacific Theatres. It was recommissioned as an advanced aviation base ship. As were most landing ship tanks of that era, it was diesel powered, which enabled it to be beached and function efficiently in shallow water. The need and the hazards of taking on water in the shallows were lessened.

The USS Tallahatchie County was one of only two steam-powered landing ship tanks. It was newer and larger than the Alameda County and was a much better ride.

Advanced aviation base ships sailed to distant shores, mostly islands, to set up advanced aviation bases that would support antisubmarine warfare squadrons, usually composed of land-based aircraft. The advanced bases had a runway and sometimes a hangar. The advanced aviation base ship would supply everything else except the ordinance, which, at many of the North Atlantic Treaty Organization bases, was stored there in advance.

The unique thing about the advanced aviation base ship was its crew, which comprised "black shoes" (sea arm/sailors), "brown shoes" (air arm/aviators), and "CBs" (Construction Battalion)—all three components of the navy.

My first trip aboard the Alameda County was memorable. Because of a limited amount of officer quarters, I bunked in the sick bay as the ship departed Naples for Souda Bay, Crete. As we left the Bay of Naples and headed south toward the Strait of Messina, the ship lost power.

I was asleep when the incident occurred. The banging of the unsecured hatch to the sick bay because of the rocking of the ship awakened me. I was holding onto the bar on the side of the bunk with my head and left shoulder hanging over the side facing the deck. My fingers were slightly numb, so I must have been holding on that way for a while. Not long after, the problem was fixed. Not the way to experience your first cruise!

USS Alameda County

Appearance of the US Department of
Defense (DOD) visual information does
not imply or constitute DOD endorsement

I also deployed with the Alameda County to Cagliari, Sardinia. We had
to drive to the base, where the air operations were conducted. In Cagliari, I
visited a conventional diesel submarine. Unlike our nuclear-powered
submarines, the quarters were close. When under way, submerged, the air
could become fowl, lending the derogatory nickname for that type vessel—a
"pig boat."

The submarine that was in port when we were there, had been banned
from major Mediterranean ports because its crew members went berserk
when they took shore leave. After spending some shore leave at the same bar
with them, I understood why. Some of the sub's senior officers were in the
same bar while their men were acting unruly. The captain of our ship was the
senior officer ashore, and he had to speak with the sub's two officers and order
them to control their crew or return to their sub. But given what they had to
endure submerged in that boat for extended periods, I could understand, but
not condone, their behavior when they were let loose ashore.

After a while, I found out that when the Alameda County was not
sailing to its advanced base destination, I could fly to that base and join the ship
there. One such time, just before the Cuban Missile Crisis, the Alameda County
was heading to Crete via the Adriatic Sea, with a port-of-call in Venice.

51

On the way from Venice to Souda Bay, the Alameda County was enveloped in a violent storm in the Adriatic Sea and was lifted on the crest of a huge wave. That wave moved suddenly from under the ship, and the ship violently dropped to the trough of the wave. The resulting impact split the hull in two places, each split extending halfway around the hull. It was a minor miracle the ship made it to Souda Bay. The captain had to beach the ship gingerly because of his fear that if he made a normal beaching, it might break up when he tried to back it off the beach. The ship had "way on" (the screws/propellers were turning) to maintain its position on the beach for the ten days we operated at Souda Bay.

After the operation, the captain backed off the beach without causing further damage. He sailed it down the bay to a drydock, where it had about one foot of clearance, and was welded back together. Once the Tallahatchie County arrived, the Alameda County was given or sold to the Italian navy. When the US Navy started to remove equipment from the ship, the Italians threatened to cancel the deal. We quickly stopped because we doubted we could ever sail it back to the US. I was always amused to see the ship, under the Italian flag, cruising around the Bay of Naples.

The Tallahatchie County was a pleasure craft compared with the Alameda County. It was longer, wider, and faster; had a deeper draft; and carried a bigger payload. She relieved the Alameda County on June 25, 1962. During the period that the Tallahatchie County was home-ported in Naples, the Cuban Missile Crisis came to fruition.

Souda Bay, Crete

For a month or more beginning in September 1962, Naval Air Facility Naples was on high alert, with marines patrolling the tarmac and the rest of the airbase carrying loaded shotguns.

USS Tallahatchie County
(USS Forestall in background)

Appearance of the US Department of Defense (DOD) visual information does not imply or constitute DOD endorsement

Even though I had a top-secret security clearance, I had no idea what was going on, but it was clear that something serious was in the wind.

Something serious was also about to take place in my personal life. I was not enjoying being a bachelor anymore. It was time for me to settle down with my one and only love, Audrey Britton.

I had participated in two weddings of my fellow officers. One was George Suchand, who married his Italian girlfriend. Once he did so, he lost his top-secret clearance and his job in the courier office. He was transferred to the military police under the naval support activities command. They have been living a wonderful life together. We remained friends and stayed in touch for many years.

Early in July 1962, I had written to Audrey reiterating why I thought we should wait to marry until after I completed my tour of duty in Italy. In that letter, I admonished her about not writing me more frequently. She had told me that she didn't write more often because she felt she didn't have much that was new to tell me. I told her to write even if her letter only said, "I love you." Within a week after posting that letter, I wrote her another letter stating that I changed my mind and I wanted us to marry that fall. I asked that she write back and give me and answer to my proposal.

My proposal letter got lost, and Audrey never received it. After several weeks, I was beside myself, and my hair began to fall out. My barber, Paul, exclaimed, "*Tenente*, you're losing your hair!" Bill McGhee, with whom I shared an apartment, observed my fallen hair in the bathroom sink and predicted that I would be bald in a month. I went to see the flight surgeon, Lieutenant Commander Phil Nyborg, and he determined my problem was psychological.

I was stubborn, and after my admonishment of Audrey about her infrequent letters, I felt that I shouldn't write her until she responded to my letter. I did not want to pressure her. Maybe she was trying to make up her mind. Because of my frustration, I wrote my mother a letter explaining the situation. Although I didn't ask her to contact Audrey, I knew she would.

After speaking with my mother, Audrey wrote me a frantic letter swearing that she never received my proposal letter, and she declared her undying love for me and her desire for us to marry as soon as possible. My hair stopped falling out within a day. I prepared for my return to New York to get married, right after my forthcoming deployment to the advanced aviation base at Souda Bay, Crete.

The Cuban Missile Crisis

I was buoyed by the thought of my impending marriage to Audrey. So much so, that I had suppressed the fact that Naval Air Facility Naples was on high alert for more than six weeks. Whatever the reason, I knew something serious was under way, and I had to prepare for my impending temporary duty assignment with the Tallahatchie County. I flew to Souda Bay, Crete, and joined the ship there.

Everything at the base was normal. I was busy providing meteorological support for two operations: one in the Mediterranean Sea between Sicily and Crete and a second in the Adriatic and Ionian Seas. Those operations were taking place as the world's first nuclear-powered aircraft carrier, the USS Enterprise, had deployed with the Sixth Fleet for the first time. That event attracted more than the usual attention from the Russian submarines, which always tracked our fleet's activities in the Mediterranean, especially during the Cold War.

At some point, our fleet became aroused about the Russian subs and the way they were tracking the Enterprise. When we could not get their sub(s) to surface (for identification purposes and, unbeknownst to me, Cuba preparing to receive Soviet missiles), our antisubmarine squadron commenced a third operation in the eastern Mediterranean with deadly intent.

The antisubmarine warfare squadron armed their P2-Vs with the deadliest depth charges in their arsenal and began a campaign to blow those subs out of the water. I have no knowledge whether these actions sunk any subs, but I am certain the sonar men on those subs suffered severe hearing loss, if nothing else. That operation went on for two days, during which I managed to get about five hours of sleep. I later learned that on the way to Souda Bay, one of the cargo vessels that the Tallahatchie County reported traveling westward in the Mediterranean was among the first to be turned back by the US naval blockade of Cuba during the crisis.

When the Enterprise's exercise ended, it sailed to the western Mediterranean, where it was relieved by another carrier. It then returned to its home port of Norfolk, Virginia. Our advanced base operation terminated, and I flew back to Naples. The next day, I began my trip to New York via military transport to get married. The crisis continued.

Given my security clearance, I could sign up as a courier and get the first flight out of Naples to Naval Air Station Port Lyautey in Kenitra, Morocco. It was my first flight on a Lockheed C-130, a four-engine turboprop cargo plane. From there, I traveled to Lajes Air Base on Terceira Island in the Atlantic's Azores archipelago.

Because the upper-level (westerly) winds were strong, instead of flying to the naval air station in Argentia, Newfoundland, we flew to Kindley Air Force Base in Bermuda. From there, it was on to Naval Station Norfolk, where we landed early in the morning.

During this trip, a superior officer challenged my authority. As a courier officer, I had specific duties and responsibilities to perform to secure the courier material. The courier is the last person to board the aircraft after verifying that the courier material has been securely loaded and locked in the aircraft's fuselage and hold. The courier is armed with a sidearm that he or she turns over to the aircraft crew after everyone is on board and the aircraft is ready for takeoff. Upon landing, the crew returns the sidearm to the courier officer before the aircraft door is opened. That officer must be the first person to depart the aircraft to assure that he is present when the aircraft's hold is unlocked, and the courier material is taken under control and signed for by the intended courier recipient.

As we landed in the Azores on the second leg of my trip home, the crew chief returned my sidearm to me as the plane was taxiing to where the passengers would deplane. A lieutenant commander, who was a passenger, decided he was going to be the first to depart the aircraft. I don't know whether he disregarded me because of his seniority or because of my race or both. But I politely declared that I, as the courier officer, would be the first person to leave the aircraft. I then loaded my sidearm and looked him straight in the eyes, daring him to deplane before me. He asked, "Are you going to shoot me?" I replied, "That will depend on you." I was the first to leave the aircraft and fulfilled my responsibility.

I don't know if I would have shot him. But our armed forces were on high alert because of the severity of the Cuban Missile Crisis. I was safeguarding the courier material in my custody.

From Norfolk, I flew commercially to New York's LaGuardia Airport. A lot was going on in that part of Queens. The airport's Central Terminal Building was under construction, and about a mile away, Shea Stadium, the future home of the New York Mets, was also being built.

After embracing my parents and greeting my friends on Washington Avenue, my next stop was to see Audrey.

We made the final plans for our wedding, which took place on Monday, October 8, 1962, at Holy Rood Episcopal Church in Upper Manhattan, a few blocks from the George Washington Bridge. The service was performed by the Reverend Ernest Davies, who had been my minister at St. Paul's Episcopal Church many years earlier.

Audrey had a lot to do to get ready. She had to rely on her father to drive her around because she couldn't drive, and she had to rely on public transportation when he was working. She was an hour late for the ceremony. My father, who was a stickler for punctuality, approached me at about the thirty-minute-late mark and said, "You know, you can leave if you want to. You've waited long enough." His comment had nothing to do with Audrey; punctuality was in his DNA. He grew to love her without reservation, as we all did.

Our wedding took place without a hitch. Rudy Gray, my godbrother, was my best man, and Betty Watkins, Audrey's best friend, was matron of honor. We spent our honeymoon in Manhattan and stayed at the Hotel Taft, just north of Times Square. Our first days as husband and wife were wonderful, and I bought her several modest gifts, which prompted her to ask, "Will you always treat me this good?" I promised her that I would and that I hoped to do even better in the future.

The next step was to get her to Italy with me via military transport, which, because of the Cuban Missile Crisis, still unbeknownst to all but a few principals in the world, would prove impossible. I made several trips to McGuire Air Force Base, and I could not get us on any flights. With my leave time running out, I had to go plan B.

I gave my father money to purchase a one-way ticket to Rome, Italy, on TWA. After I got back, I would meet Audrey upon her arrival. I traveled to Naval Station Norfolk and used my courier status to get back to COMFAIRMED. I travelled to Norfolk by Greyhound bus via the Chesapeake Bay Bridge Tunnel, which had recently opened.

When I got to Naval Station Norfolk, staying in the bachelor officer quarters awaiting assignment to a flight that would get me to Italy, I finally learned what was going on in Cuba.

Audrey called me, in a panic, and asked if I had heard President Kennedy's speech? She related the contents of the speech with emphasis on the president's ultimatum to Nikita Khrushchev, leader of the USSR. Audrey and I had only been married about ten days, and she thought she would never see me again. We were on the brink of a nuclear war, and she thought the world was about to be obliterated. I believed we would survive the crisis, and I assured her we'd be together again soon. I thanked God that President Kennedy and Secretary Khrushchev resolved that crisis.

After a few days, I was on my way back across the Atlantic Ocean as the courier officer on a cargo plane, headed for Italy via North Africa. As soon as I got back, I notified my father and Audrey and arranged for her to fly to Rome.

Before I left New York for Norfolk, I gave Audrey some money for personal and travel needs. I also briefed her on all the things that could go wrong on her trip and what to do if they did, especially if I could not meet her at the airport in Rome. I even gave her a *gettone*, a slug-like token that was used to make telephone calls in public telephone booths, and the phone number of the US Embassy. Audrey had never traveled anywhere outside the New York area by herself, and this was going to be her first trip outside the US.

I got to Rome early and was elated to see Audrey deplane. She was one of the first passengers off the plane, and I watched her walk across the tarmac and enter the terminal. That was the last I saw of her for a long time. She got disoriented in the customs and immigration area and after completing the process walked the wrong way. I was about to lose it when she finally walked out the door. She was the last passenger from her flight to leave the immigration area.

After a scenic drive, we arrived at my apartment on Via Scipioni Capece in Naples. As I introduced her to her new environment, I asked her how much money she had left. She told me five dollars. I gasped and repeated, "Five dollars! What would you have done if I wasn't able to meet you?" She casually looked at me, smiling, and replied, "You met me, didn't you?" She never doubted that I would be there.

The Cuban Missile Crisis was over, and we were moving on. Nevertheless, the tension took a while to dissipate. My major mission was to get Audrey settled and to acclimate to being a husband. It wasn't a difficult transition for me at all. I was ready. It was so good having her with me. I regretted not having done it sooner.

I took her to COMFAIRMED and introduced her to Lieutenant Donovan, our personnel officer. We obtained a military dependents ID for her to be eligible for the benefits, privileges, and protections due an official navy dependent. Next, I introduced her to Bill and B. B. McGhee, George and Lilliana Suchand, other officers, and my "Italian brother," Antonio Fusco.

Antonio Fusco and Pepino

My Italian Brother

When I first arrived in Naples, I resided in a small *pensione*, a boarding house, not too far from the city center. It was below a section of Naples named Vomero, which is on a plateau and overlooks the Bay of Naples. It could be reached from where I lived by a *funicolare*, a cable car. It was a section with many middle-class inhabitants and known for its Vomero women, reputed to be the prettiest women in Naples.

In June 1961, I moved to an apartment in Vomero on Via Felipe Pallizzi, which had a magnificent view of the bay, Mount Vesuvius, the Sorrento Peninsula, the Isle of Capri, and Marechiaro. There, I met Antonio, who owned the garage in the building adjacent to mine.

I had acquired a car, a Morris Minor convertible, which I was advised not to park on the street overnight. Given the proximity of Antonio's garage, I willingly parked it there. Five days later, I fractured and dislocated my right ankle playing softball on the COMFAIRMED staff's team and was hospitalized for several days. When I returned to my apartment, fitted with a long leg cast up to my groin, Antonio sought me out because I had not come to retrieve my car for several days. He was shocked to see me in that condition, and he visited me frequently. Our friendship grew with each passing day.

Aside from my housekeeper, Teresa, who had started working for me only a few days earlier, Lieutenant Alex Bryant, the brother-in-law of one of my lifelong friends; Tommy Barnes; Antonio; and Antonio's friend Armando, who worked in a hotel and spoke good English, were my main human contacts the first four weeks at home. My proficiency in Italian increased.

My hospitalization had a few ironic twists. The first began when I visited a hospitalized American civilian contractor for the US Navy, Frank Bishop. He had contracted mononucleosis. While there, the only seat available was in a wheelchair, which I sat in because he had another visitor. As we talked, a nurse entered his room and ask me, "Are you the patient?" I said no and pointed to Frank saying, "He's the patient." The next night is when I broke my ankle, and I became the patient!

The evening I was admitted into the hospital, the duty doctor was Captain Isenberg. He was reputed to be the navy's leading orthopedic surgeon. But as the duty doctor, he had three women in labor whose babies he had to deliver. All he could do for me was put my ankle and lower leg in a pillow splint. It would have to be set the next day. I laid there and tried to sleep and deal with the pain, which began to intensify once the pillow splint was applied. I had rarely, if ever, slept on my back, so my sleep was fitful.

Just before I drifted to sleep, I got a roommate, a navy chaplain. He was brought in, hunched over in severe pain from bursitis in his right shoulder. He was heartened when he discovered the duty doctor was Captain Isenberg, who had treated him when he'd had a similar attack ten years prior in Norfolk.

The next morning, I was dreaming that someone or something was attacking me. I fought off the assailant (in my dream) by kicking him with my right leg, which was in the splint. I let out a scream, and the attending nurse and someone else came racing into the room. They found me in excruciating pain and the chaplain laughing his ass off. The chaplain, himself still in pain, thought it was hilarious that I "rose a foot off the bed" when I kicked in my dream.

When Captain Isenberg got me into the operating room, the anesthesiologist had difficulty giving me a spinal tap, so the captain told her to put me to sleep. I was told that the captain had the surgical pins ready to insert into my ankle. But after some time, he had manipulated the broken bones into the proper position, making the pins unnecessary. I was thankful for his skill. When I awoke, I found my right leg in a cast that extended up to my groin. I would get a heel attached two weeks later, after my first follow-up examination. I had to learn to use crutches in a hurry, but I didn't learn to use them skillfully soon enough.

I had visited Frank on Sunday afternoon, broke my ankle Monday evening, had corrective surgery on Tuesday morning, and was discharged on Friday. On Saturday morning, I stood on my terrace admiring the beauty of the bay, and I saw the USS Forrestal anchored in the bay. My VAW-24 buddies were about to pay a debt. They owed me a party—long leg cast, crutches, and all.

My only means of transportation was Alex, whom I presumed would be going to the Officers Club at the Allied Forces Southern Europe Headquarters in Bagnoli, just outside Naples. He and his wife took me to the club. I picked out a comfortable lounge chair with a low cocktail table in front of it so I could park my cast on it. It was the only way I could sit down because I couldn't bend my knee. I felt helpless, which would prove to be disadvantageous when John Fox and crew would discover me. I was only one day out of a hospital bed and had not yet mastered my crutches.

John walked into the bar and saw me with my leg propped up on the cocktail table. He greeted me with rancor and affection and called the rest of the guys.

I had already become friends with the bartenders at the club. I was easily recognizable because there were few officers of African descent in the US Navy and in Naples. I drank scotch on the rocks, and liquor was cheap at military facilities. Whenever I ordered a drink, the bartenders would always pour me a double without me asking, so I had to be aware of my consumption. When John reappeared with the guys, he was not aware of that and would not have cared had he known.

They ordered round after round. When I said I'd had enough, they threatened to pour it down my throat. I beckoned to Alex to take me home. I thanked them and bid them goodbye, never hearing from or seeing them again except for John, who called me out of the blue fifty-four years later and asked how I was doing. The conversation was short, and he didn't leave a number.

I felt that I had control of my faculties, but I was more than slightly drunk. Upon arriving home, Alex helped me out of the car, and as I attempted to mount the curb, I tried to put my right foot up first, I guess out of habit, and banged the bottom of the cast on the curb's edge. I must have awakened half of Via Pallizzi with my scream.

Alex helped me to my bedroom, and I quickly faded. The next morning, I woke up, with my hands folded on my chest, fully clothed, and I wondered whether I was dead or alive. I realized I was living because I had to pee so bad. I barely made it to the bathroom.

Antonio was the first to visit me after my sojourn to the Officers Club and visited many times thereafter. He observed that my mother would frequently send me a package of one of her specialties, coconut bread, which he became addicted to. One of his first questions when he entered the apartment was, *"Hai ricevuto il pane del tuo mamma?"* ("Did you receive your mama's bread?") If I answered yes, he would head for the kitchen and cut a slice for himself. He compared it with *panettone*, a fluffy Italian bread with raisins.

After two weeks, Captain Isenberg reexamined my ankle, which was healing well, and determined he could put a rubber heel on it. It made me more mobile. He told me that as my circulation improved, because of my increased mobility, the leg might start to itch. He warned me, "Don't scratch it. You will regret it!"

About three weeks later, the itch got to me, and I scratched, just a little. I used a metal clothes hanger to reach inside the cast below the knee.

I was standing on my terrace, holding the railing, when I started scratching. The more I scratched, the more places on my leg began to itch. I reached the stage where I couldn't bear the torment any longer. I tried not to scream out loud. I threw down the hanger and squeezed the railing so hard that my hands became numb. After what seemed like forever, the itch subsided. I cursed myself for doing what I did and vowed I would never be such a smart ass again.

The rubber heel allowed me to perform some modified work at Naval Air Facility Naples. I could also jam myself into Antonio's Fiat 500 by sliding the passenger seat all the way back with bottom of the cast firmly pressed against the partition just below the dashboard. Antonio took me to Portici, where I met his father and other family members. I got to know his wife, Cecilia, and infant son, Fabio. When I returned from the US after my marriage, he was one of the first people to meet Audrey.

During my recovery, my Morris Minor got totaled. Alex had asked to borrow it to travel up north to Camp Darby in the Pisa-Livorno area of western Italy, primarily to shop at the large army exchange there. On his return to Naples, he ran off the road near Civitavecchia, and the car hit a tree. His son, a chubby toddler, was thrown through the convertible's roof and landed on his stomach on a soft piece of terrain. Cars did not have seat belts in the early 1960s, so they were fortunate not to be seriously injured.

Because of the legal agreement between the US and Italy, I couldn't replace the car until it was exported out of the country. To do that, I had to rent a railroad freight car, onto which the wreck was loaded and brought to Naples. It was then loaded onto a barge, which was taken out beyond twenty miles from the coast and dumped into the ocean. This was only possible because the COMFAIRMED administrative officer was sympathetic to my plight and partially disabled condition and opted to have it done for me.

Alex promised to pay me for the loss, but he left Naples and the navy without fulfilling his promise. When I returned to New York after completing my active duty service in May 1963, I had to take him to small claims court and sue him for the money. He acknowledged the obligation to the court and was ordered to pay me, which he did.

My replacement car, an Opel, met a similar fate, except this time, I was driving. I was on the way home from the Officers Club one Saturday night when a local driver failed to yield the right-of-way as he was leaving the soccer stadium parking area. He broadsided me on the passenger side, rolling me over, I believe, twice. I saw the vehicle coming and managed to brace myself for the impact.

As my car rolled over, I saw flashes of light, which led me to believe the car had caught on fire, so when it came to an upright stop, I jumped out. The car was a mess, but it was not burning. The flashes of light I thought might be flames, I determined, were the street lights illuminating the inside of the vehicle as it rolled over. I had left the club early that night. I didn't feel like drinking any alcohol, so all I had was Coca-Cola. I was stone-cold sober. My injury was minor, just few fragments of glass in my hair. The next day, my left arm and shoulder were sore. When I bought my next car, another Opel, I took it to the parachute loft and had them install seat belts.

I picked up Audrey in Rome in the second Opel. We visited Florence, Pisa, Venice, Siena, Capri, and Positano. During the time Audrey was with me in Italy, I did not have to go on any exercises that took me away from Naples for an extended period.

Italy was a great experience for both of us. It was topped off when we returned home first class from Naples to New York aboard the SS Constitution. It was the first sailing experience on an ocean liner for both of us. I had procured several visitors passes for my friends who were seeing us off, which included Bill and B. B. McGhee, George and Lilliana Suchand, and Antonio and Cecilia, who was pregnant with their second child, Paola.

We were having a good time at our bon voyage party, but I was concerned because Antonio hadn't arrived. He was there but, unbeknownst to him, a few days before we were scheduled to embark, the administrative department in charge of our travel changed my cabin because they wanted to accommodate a navy officer with a family. Using my cabin allowed them to do that, even though it was a downgrade for him. But I didn't know where I was going to be lodged in time to get new visitors passes for my guest.

Antonio and Cecilia were waiting on a lower deck at my original assigned cabin until a crew member who spoke Italian found out what was going on and brought them up to my new cabin. Our time together was shortened, but I was glad for what little time we had. It would be twenty-two years before we would see each other in person again. We kept in contact because I made the effort to learn to read and write Italian, not just speak it. I believed I was going to meet people I would want to keep in my life after I departed.

We sailed away that night bound for New York with ports-of-call at Genoa, Italy; Nice, France; Barcelona, Spain; Algeciras, Morocco; and Funchal, Madeira Islands. We saw many sites, but the most memorable was Funchal, a hilly, mountainous island, where the basic downhill transportation was wooden sleds with greased wooden runners known as "the Monte Toboggan." We took an exhilarating ride down steep and winding roads. The sleds were controlled by men dressed in clothes traditional to the island. They wore rubber boots, which functioned as the sled's brakes.

After departing the Madeira Islands, we sailed three days to New York. Our parents were waiting to greet us. My brother-in-law, Donald Hinson, and Audrey's father, Theodore Britton, were there to whisk us home. After we collected our luggage, Audrey's parents hustled her into their car and drove off. It was as if she had been kidnapped.

In hindsight, I could understand their desire to find out how Audrey's married life was shaping up. I am sure they were curious to know how I was treating her, providing for her, whether she was happy, and so on. They missed her, especially her mother. But they hadn't told me they were taking her to their house. Shortly after we got to my house on Washington Avenue, I had to call them and ask, "What did you do with my wife?"

That was the only time I ever had to fire a shot across their bow. I had to get the message across that we were in charge of our lives and that I was the head of our household. They were both caring and considerate parents who loved, and wanted the best, for their only daughter. I learned to love them without reservation, and they loved me back in the same manner.

Lesson Learned Along the Way
19. Don't be a smart ass. Be receptive to advice from those who know.

STATION: WILLIAMS BRIDGE

We were back at 1516 Washington Avenue, living with my parents. It was nice to see and be among many of my childhood friends, but it was clear that I had to extricate myself from the neighborhood if I was going to progress. I knew that if my parents moved with me, I would then have the option of visiting the neighborhood if I wanted to, not because I was obligated to return because my parents still lived there.

I had my sights set on the Williamsbridge section of the north Bronx, where I frequently visited "Aunt" Lee (Halliburton) and a few acquaintances when I was growing up. When Uncle Lewis and Aunt Muriel moved from our Washington Avenue apartment, they moved into the small apartment on the ground level of Aunt Lee's house at 726 East 217th Street. I visited them many times.

Once, my grandmother Mum, and my cousin Linda, who at the time was about two years old and I about ten, were visiting there. Linda and I were playing with a ball on the sidewalk in front of the house. The ball got loose and rolled into the street. I told Linda to stay and that I would get it. As I waited for a few cars to pass, Linda came streaking by me, determined to get the ball herself. I reached out and was barely able to grab her as the cars rolled by. Mum must not have noticed what happened because neither of us got scolded or whacked.

My housing search came to fruition when I found a five-room apartment that was advertised in the *Bronx Home News*, a Bronx newspaper affiliated with, and later acquired by, the *New York Post*. It was on the second floor and had three bedrooms with a small sunporch adjacent to the living room. It was just right for us. 748 East 219th Street was half a block from the 219th Street station on the city's White Plains Road train line and two short blocks from St. George's Episcopal Church, which we would attend. The

Harlem Line station, Williams Bridge, was at Gun Hill Road, four stations and four miles north of the old Claremont Parkway station.

It was the first time in my life, excluding naval duty transfers, that I had ever moved. It felt like I had escaped, broken the chains that bound me. I was moving up, and the sky was the limit!

Lesson Learned Along the Way
20. When involved with children, expect the unexpected. They will find trouble.

The US Weather Bureau Revisited

I notified the Weather Bureau in May 1963 that I was separated from active duty. The bureau was obligated to hold a position open for me for four years because I was officially on military leave as a government employee. After five or six weeks, they assigned me to the Overseas Briefing Office at Idlewild International Airport, which became John F. Kennedy International Airport (JFK). It was a meteorologist (GS-9) position, the maximum level I would have attained, considering my military forecasting experience, if I had remained at the bureau.

The meteorologist in charge was Milton Werblin. Two of the meteorologists on the staff were also graduates of CCNY, one of whom was a classmate of mine and a US Air Force veteran. Both (Takis Abramediis and Nicholas Condos) were of Greek descent. Larry Morley, a New York University graduate and an Irishman to the hilt, was the other member of our team.

The Overseas Briefing Office provided weather briefings and maps and charts to all international flights departing JFK. The job was easier for me because I didn't have additional local and regional forecasting duties to perform like I did when I was in the navy. Most of my briefing were not made to the pilots but to their operations personnel. But we were also responsible for all the weather observations for the airport. At night, you were normally on duty alone, and when the weather was bad, keeping up with the observations, combined with your regular briefing duties, kept you busy.

My biggest adjustment was getting acclimated to working shifts. Because I was not a big sleeper and could rarely sleep during the day, the midnight shift was the most difficult of the three for me—not the shift itself, but the day after I finished it. My sleep was always fragmented. I could only sleep for three hours or so in the morning and found it difficult to go to sleep for a few hours in the evening before my shift. Otherwise, I could manage my time around the morning and evening shifts. I committed to other activities, such as substitute teaching, learning the insurance business, fulfilling my US Navy active reserve obligation, and spending time with Audrey.

At JFK, I met a male Alitalia flight steward who lived in Naples. I told him about Antonio, whom he contacted and informed that he had met me. Not too long thereafter, Antonio managed to have him bringing me gifts on a couple of occasions. I rarely reciprocated because I didn't want to take advantage of him or cause him any trouble, even though he didn't seem to mind.

Overseas Briefing Office

I experienced many amusing and a few sad events during my time at JFK.

There was the time that I had to work twenty-three hours straight because a major snowstorm had paralyzed the New York area, and everything was shut down. Passengers were stranded in all the terminals. The parking lots where full of cars surrounded by more than twenty inches of snow. No one could enter or leave the airport, and most of the restaurants ran out of food. When my relief finally arrived, I still had to stay awhile because everything was so disrupted that it took all of us to get the briefing office functioning properly.

Another event occurred because I could speak Italian. To make our weather observations, we had to walk up a flight of stairs to our "penthouse" on the roof of the International Arrivals Building, where our office was located. From there, adjacent to the observation deck, we could view the entire sky in addition to the tarmac of the east wing of the building, where many incoming international flights deplaned their passengers. There were no jetways, so passengers walked down moveable stairs, crossed the tarmac, and entered the east wing immigration area. People who came to the observation deck could see passengers deplane.

One day, while taking an observation, an Alitalia flight was about to arrive at its assigned spot on the east wing tarmac. Running slowly in my direction was a woman who appeared excited. Our penthouse was about four feet higher than the observation deck. She stopped in front of me, and looking up, asked, "*Qual e la porta del volo Alitalia?*" ("What gate does the Alitalia flight arrive?") I responded, "*Impresa al cancello cinque.*" ("It arrives at gate five.")

She thanked me and trotted off toward gate five, but she stopped, turned around, and came back to me looking surprised. She asked, "*Sei Italiano?*" ("Are you Italian?") I responded with a broad smile, "*Si, sono un*

Napolitano!" ("Yes, I am a Napolitan!") I couldn't stop laughing as she walked away toward gate five saying "No, no, no, no" in disbelief.

One of the saddest events I experienced at the Overseas Briefing Office was on Friday, November 22, 1963. I was sitting at a high desk next to a window, preparing flight briefing folders for flights scheduled to depart that afternoon. The radio was on. Shortly after 12:30 p.m., a piercing alarm came blaring over the airwave. It stimulated my worst thoughts and fears.

Most of us were aware that President Kennedy had traveled to Dallas, Texas, that day. As soon as I heard that alarm, before any voice came on to make an announcement, I blurted out, "Something has happened to the president! The [stock] market is going to crash!" No sooner had the words come out of my mouth when an announcer stated that the president had been shot and was being rushed to the hospital.

While I worked at the Overseas Briefing Office, I was also fulfilling my US Navy active reserve duty obligation at Naval Air Station New York, located on Floyd Bennett Field in Brooklyn. The US Coast Guard was also located there. One of the coast guard officers stationed there was a lieutenant I met when I was on active duty, stationed at Naval Air Station Quonset Point. He took me on my first flight in a helicopter. Several times, I flew with him on patrols over New York City, Long Island Sound, and northern New Jersey.

Milton Werblin, meteorologist in charge of the Overseas Briefing Office, was accommodating in helping me fulfill reserve obligations by arranging my schedule so that I would work the evening shifts on the weekends that I had naval reserve duty. Because Floyd Bennett Field is only fourteen miles west of JFK, it took me about twenty minutes to drive from there to the office. I would return to Naval Air Station New York and sleep at the Officers Club on Saturday night, fulfill my reserve duty on Sunday, work my weather bureau shift that evening, and go home.

On one of those reserve duty weekends, while I was in the Weather Office at Naval Air Station New York, and in walked Lieutenant Commander Joseph Stephen Henriquez for a weather briefing. Henriquez was one of the navy's most accomplished aviators and was black. I had met him at Naval Air Facility Naples, where he, Alex Bryant, and I were the only three black naval officers in that area. It was a delight to greet him, but that day would be the last time I would see him.

He always exuded self-confidence and professionalism in appearance and performance. His military bearing was superb. He was admired by most, loved by many, and respected by all his fellow officers and enlisted men.

He could be amusing and playful. Several times, at navy recreational events or on the base when he came upon me in relative isolation, he would walk up to me and, with a big smile, whisper, sometimes in my ear, "Hello, Blacky!" It always caused me to let out a robust guffaw. We were always aware of the weight that, as black officers, we always carried. The act, for us, was pressure relief.

I was saddened when I read of his death in the January 1967 issue of *Ebony* magazine. The editorial was extensive, and among the many photos, the one captioned "Deceased Navy Pilot, Henriquez, Gets High Award," showing Joe's wife and children viewing the Distinguished Flying Cross medals, touched me the most deeply. The text read as follows:

> Vice President Humphrey presented the Distinguished Flying Cross to the widow of one of the Navy's greatest fliers, the late Lt. Comdr. Joseph Stephen Henriquez, in Washington. The Harlem product, who was on his way to becoming the Navy's first Negro squadron commander, was killed last summer during a takeoff from the carrier Constellation in the South China Sea while enroute on his 23rd mission over North Vietnam. When Navy brass mailed the DFC to the family, Vice President Humphrey learned of the protocol slip and asked that he be allowed to present the award in a ceremony in his Capitol Hill office.

Joe's navy nickname was "Fighting Joe Henriquez." He had many flying hours and participated in the Mercury Test Project, the precursor to our space program. He could have become one of our nation's first astronauts, but his height ultimately disqualified him.

Milton's Leadership

Generally, working with my fellow meteorologists was a pleasure. We had an admirable comradery, and rarely was there friction between us. Teamwork and mutual respect was the norm, and Milton Werblin, our meteorologist-in-charge, set the tone.

We were usually working alone in the office after 6:00 p.m., but it was busy. Most evening international flights to Europe departed JFK between 5:00 p.m. and 11:00 p.m., with most bunched up between 7:00 p.m. and 9:30 p.m. Several airline operations staff would come to the office during that same period to pick up their flight folders. Sometimes, we would review flight forecasts with them.

Several nights, while on evening shifts, Mike (I can't recall his surname), who worked for Aer Lingus, Ireland's national airline, came to the office to pick up a flight forecast. I was seated on a high chair at the workstation, which was a wide and high table.

The first night on the shift, Mike came to the office and greeted me with a hard slap on my upper back. I didn't say anything, but he noticed that my reaction was not one of approval. On the subsequent night, he repeated the action, this time accompanied by a snarling, mumbled remark that I couldn't understand, but my instincts made me feel that it wasn't complimentary. I asked him what he said as he walked toward the door. He stopped in the doorway and turned around mouthing words that I interpreted as being some type of racial comment. He was purposeful not to make what he said audible. His facial expressions throughout each encounter bordered on threatening.

The next day, I discussed the situation with Milton, explaining to him that I couldn't state with certainty what Mike said to me, but it was hostile and inappropriate. Milton did not give me the third degree but asked me only a few clarifying questions. He was disturbed about what had taken place, and he took immediate action. He was not about to permit anyone to disrespect his staff, and he went to Aer Lingus and read them the riot act. He banned Mike from entering the Overseas Briefing Office.

It reinforced the high regard I held for him, and I believe it did so for the others with whom I worked. He would support me many months later when I applied for another position in the Eastern Regional Office.

Fatherhood

In late 1963, we discovered that Audrey was pregnant. She had chronic ulcerated colitis, but it was well managed, and her pregnancy went well until it was time to give birth. Our family doctor, Maxwell Ballen, who, although not an obstetrician, had delivered several of the Sobers family children, including my nephew, Donald, and my cousin, Linda, oversaw Audrey's prenatal care.

On Wednesday morning, July 29, 1964, Audrey called me at the office to tell me delivery time was approaching. I rushed home and took her to Lebanon Hospital on Mount Eden Avenue and Grand Concourse in the Bronx, one of the city's newest and finest hospitals. She would remain in labor until the next afternoon, primarily because our son had moved his head and would not, or could not, straighten it out. Finally, Dr. Ballen called in a surgeon, who delivered Loren Scott Sobers by caesarian section. But more trepidation would come.

Dr. Ballen assisted in the delivery, and when it was over, he told me that I had a son who he described as "pink" and healthy looking. Ballen was pleased. After checking on Audrey, who went to a surgical ward rather than the maternity ward because she had developed a fever, I went to see my son.

I was pleased to see him but was alarmed. He appeared to be normal in every respect but one. His color was not pink. He was a light, putrid brown, bordering on green. Around 11:00 p.m., I received a call from a pediatric specialist informing me that he had been called in to treat Loren, who had developed hyaline membrane disease, now commonly called respiratory distress syndrome. There was no known cure for the condition.

Early the next morning, the specialist told me that Loren had pulled through and was doing fine. He considered us fortunate because President Kennedy's baby had died shortly after being born with the same condition. The specialist said, "It just goes to show you that having money isn't everything.

They have plenty, and it wasn't enough to save their son." It was, for me, a lesson: the only priceless possession we have is our health.

When I went to see Loren, I saw Muriel Bell, whom I knew from my vacations to Paradise Farm, a resort in the Shawangunk Range of the Catskill Mountains in Cuddebackville, New York, owned and operated by a black family headed by Sally and Jimmy Walker. We shrieked out each other's names. I had not seen Muriel Bell since the summer of 1958, and when Dr. Ballen instructed me to ask for "Nurse Bell," I had no idea that she was the head nurse of the nursery. When I first met her in the mid-fifties, her reputation as a nurse was formidable. Whatever anxieties that remained with me regarding Loren's care ceased, and I assured Audrey that he was in excellent hands.

Loren's hyaline membrane disease episode had a few ramifications that had lifelong effects. A child psychologist later diagnosed that the hyaline membrane disease contributed to his emotional development being out of sync with his mental and physical development.

It didn't help that Audrey didn't get to see and hold him until he was ten days old. She was beginning to think that she hadn't given birth. I had to call Dr. Ballen and protest the forced separation to get them to take Audrey down to the nursery to see her son. I will always remember the delight in her face and the loving warmth that she radiated during her first encounter with Loren. She was so pleased and proud! That was the first time we were together as a family.

Lesson Learned Along the Way
21. The only priceless possession we have is our health.

Introduction to Entrepreneurship

When you work rotating shifts, you have time to pursue other interests. I used my time to become licensed in insurance. I was introduced to life insurance sales by a friend and associate of my godfather, Alfred Gray, who was the most significant mentor in my life.

"Gray," as my father and I referred to him, was a New York City policeman. He had an outstanding record and never fired his weapon in the line of duty. He exuded the highest moral standards and integrity of anyone I have ever known. There is no person I have respected more.

He introduced me to personal finance, and through him, I made my first investment in a mutual fund before my eighteenth birthday.

After Audrey and I returned to the US, I spoke to Gray about purchasing life insurance. He asked Lee Kobrin, his friend and associate, to meet with me and present me with policy options. I expressed interest in his products and what he did. He offered to train and sponsor me so I could obtain my life insurance and accident and health insurance licenses. That was my entry into entrepreneurship.

We collaborated on other opportunities, and I completed the insurance course of the Sobelsohn School in March 1965. I later passed the New York state exam for my general insurance license.

Through Lee Kobrin, I met David Kaplan of David Kaplan Insurance Agency, a prominent general insurance broker. He offered me a desk in his office, and I went on to form my first formal business, W. A. Sobers Associates Inc.

I set aside and saved all the income I earned from my insurance commissions to purchase my first house in April 1966. The house, 3352 DeReimer Avenue in the Baychester section of the Bronx, was a detached, single-family dwelling. It was compact, yet spacious. We had a nice backyard with three dwarf peach trees, rose bushes, and forsythias. The small front yard had a crab apple tree.

Tragedy and Recovery

When we returned to the US in May 1963, we reenrolled Audrey in the clinic at Jacobi/Bronx Municipal Hospital, where we met Dr. Sidney Gutstein. Audrey had been making clinic visits there for more than two years. Doctors there considered her an example of how a person with chronic ulcerative colitis could live a normal life with the proper medical care. But in February 1966, a barium enema x-ray exam indicated a serious blockage in her intestine. She needed an immediate operation to correct the condition.

The operation was performed at the Albert Einstein Medical College Hospital, which was affiliated with Jacobi. The surgeon performed an ileostomy, a surgical operation in which a piece of the ileum is diverted to an artificial opening in the abdominal wall. Audrey had to wear a colostomy bag for the rest of her life because all of her large intestine and part of her small intestine was removed. The surgeon told me we would have to wait and see whether the operation removed all of her cancer.

Her operation took place when we lived on 219th Street, before we bought our house. During that period, Audrey noticed a young black man who frequently passed by our building on the way to his house on the other side of the street. While she was recuperating from the operation, she was surprised to see him walk into her hospital room one day, dressed in his laboratory coat, and requesting permission to draw her blood specimen. He was Benjamin Franklin Jones, fondly referred to as Ben, who would become my closest and dearest friend.

Ben was a hematologist and joined Albert Einstein Medical College Hospital after several years of work at the Bronx VA Hospital. He lived in an apartment in the house of Frank Flowers, an acquaintance of my father. Ben told me that four of the sixteen or so lymph nodes tested in Audrey were cancerous, but I was determined that our lives would proceed as normal, and it did for about a year.

During that year, I applied for a new position as a technical specialist for the facilities section of the engineering branch in the eastern region. It carried a higher pay grade than my current position but was a meteorological technician position, not a meteorologist position. My current position was as a meteorologist in a lower pay scale, but I ranked higher and was paid more than a meteorological technician of the same pay grade.

The head of the section, Jim McCloy, tried to prevent me from getting the position, saying that I did not have enough experience, which was garbage. Between my naval service, my degree, and two years of pre-engineering studies, I was more than qualified. I had even trained two meteorological technicians at the Overseas Briefing Office. Any technician with my qualifications would be a meteorologist.

When McCloy stated his position, I said that if I didn't get the position, I would fight the decision. I informed Milton Werblin about what had occurred and said, "If I don't get that position, they'd better have a better answer than the one McCloy gave me because I won't stand by without a fight!"

Once again, Milton demonstrated his leadership. He spoke with Silvio Simplicio, director of the eastern region. The position was important to me because it would allow me to work days on a regular basis and be more available for Audrey and Loren. I don't know what Milton told Silvio, but within a day or two, McCloy told me I had been selected for the job.

The other significant event that year was that I began my graduate education at Baruch College of the City University of New York. Earlier in the year, the Veterans Administration announced that post–Korean War veterans would qualify for education benefits. That action, in conjunction with working days in my new position, allowed me to pursue a master's degree in business administration, with a concentration in international business.

I took a "half program" each semester, at night, for six years. Because I didn't have any undergraduate courses I could transfer for credit, I had to take the equivalent of an undergraduate business curriculum before I could begin my graduate work to earn my master's degree, which I completed in June 1972.

Life became brittle in the spring of 1967. Audrey's symptoms reappeared in March. I had to rush her to the hospital in April, where she had a second abdominal operation. The cancer had returned. I questioned the surgeon about the operation's outcome. He predicted that Audrey had, maybe, three months to live.

While spending time with Audrey, she asked me, "Wayne, did I really have to have that first operation?" I assured her that it had been necessary. She was always aware of the complications of her illness, but she never dwelled on the fact that twenty percent of ulcerative colitis cases became malignant. Once, early in our marriage, she said that she sometimes thought she might die young. My response was that I would always love her, no matter what.

When I left her, I went to my parent's house. I cried as I shared the devastating news with my mother. I had to make some decisions. I wanted the remaining months of Audrey's life to be normal and worry free.

My sister, Jean, had already stepped up and taken care of Loren whenever a crisis with Audrey occurred. Jean was a teacher and was on maternity leave at the time. Her third child, Lisa, was fourteen months younger than Loren, and Lori, Jean's second child, had recently turned seven. My nephew, Donald, Jean's oldest, was twelve. Loren was welcomed into a familiar and warm environment.

I decided I would not tell anyone except my parents, my sister, and my insurance partner Lee Kobrin about Audrey's condition. I knew Ben probably knew Audrey's situation. I did not want relatives, friends, and others calling or coming around upsetting our home. When Audrey did come home, she didn't act like she was about to die, and I didn't treat her that way. She was religious and if she thought her death was imminent, I believed her faith in God would see her through. The only regret that she verbalized was that she wasn't able to take care of her son.

Life went on. I finished my first semester at school. I was not thrilled with the way Jim McCloy was using my skills at work, given my situation at home, but I tolerated it. Near the end of the month, Audrey and I went out to a Japanese restaurant for dinner. She had difficulty digesting her meal. Another evening, we went to see the movie *Dr. Zhivago*, which we both enjoyed. On July 30, 1967, Loren's third birthday, I took Audrey to the hospital for the last time.

She had her third operation to unblock what little intestine she had left. She was one of the first patients to receive chemotherapy, which was in its early experimental stage. She appeared to be improving, so much so that we talked about her coming home. I got Loren into the hospital to see her before she took a turn for the worse. Her grandparents flew in from Los Angeles to see her. She was dwindling away to nothing.

On Friday, September 8, the hospital moved Audrey into a private room. When I arrived to see her, she showed me around the room like it was a new house she had purchased. She didn't know that they moved her so that she would die in private and not upset her roommate when she did.

I spent as much time as possible with her. Ben tried to get me to take a break and asked me to go with him and two of his friends to a New York Giants preseason football game at Princeton University. He thought it would be good for me to get away. I reluctantly agreed, but I began to regret my decision. What if Audrey passed while I was attending a football game seventy miles away? I was angry and disappointed for consenting to go. Fortunately, I didn't lose her that day.

When we got to Princeton, the roads were packed, we missed the kickoff, and we discovered the game was sold out. We turned around, after watching a car crash into a telephone pole, and returned to the Bronx. I rushed to Audrey's side, relieved she was still with us.

When I arrived the next day, Sunday, September 10, 1967, I could sense that Audrey was slipping. Her grandmother and her father came to visit her that day. Several days earlier, her mother had left her room crying, stating, "I thought that I could do anything for my child, but I can't stand to see her wasting away anymore." She never saw her alive again.

I remained next to Audrey the entire afternoon. Days earlier, she had asked me, "If I die, will you put Loren up for adoption?" The question shocked me. I told her, "He's our son. I would never even consider anything like that." Then she asked me, "If I die, will you marry again?" I told her that I never gave any thought to anything like that. Then she said, "I want you to marry again."

I was standing next to the head of her bed. The gate on the side of her bed was up, and I wasn't aware enough to lower it. I was reaching around it to hold her the best that I could, my hand on the back of her right shoulder, slightly behind her neck. She was delirious, maybe even semiconscious, when she said, "I'm dying." Those were her last words. Seconds later, her eyes closed, and her head rolled over to her right. I called the nurse, and when they asked me to leave the room, I knew she was gone.

I went to the waiting room and told her father and grandmother that Audrey had died. As I was leaving the hospital, her cousin, Jon Williams, was racing up the steps to see her. I told him he was too late.

She was born on Sunday, March 17, 1940, and died on Sunday, September 10, 1967. Several days earlier, when I told her father, Theodore Britton, that her prognosis was dire, he asked me, "How long did you know she was dying?" I replied that her surgeon told me in April. Theodore said, "I'm glad you didn't tell me."

Audrey's funeral was well attended, but Loren was not there. It is one of the few decisions I've made that I regret. It negatively affected his development into his early teens. My sister believed his attendance at the funeral might be too traumatic for him. I wanted him to attend, but I went along with her suggestion. All my subsequent efforts to help him understand her passing were insufficient. The long-term result was that he didn't achieve adequate closure.

When I remarried two years later, Loren believed his new mommy would also disappear. It was another obstacle he had to overcome. But his new mommy astutely interpreted the signs of his attitudinal and physical behavior and correctly concluded that he had a psychological problem that required attention. With the love and support of family, and the professional therapy he received, his problems were addressed and ultimately resolved.

Lesson Learned Along the Way
22. When logic is foggy, follow your instincts, trust your gut!

Cutting the Umbilical Cord

My father and his older brother, Stephan, arrived in New York from Barbados aboard the SS Vandyck on October 13, 1923. He was fourteen and a half years old, and Uncle Steve was a month short of his sixteenth birthday. My grandmother ordered dad and Uncle Steve to get jobs.

Barbados has a 98 percent literacy rate. Though neither my father nor Uncle Steve had completed high school, which at the time was not uncommon, both were well educated for their age and era. Daddy was a mason and shoe salesman and held various jobs in the garment industry, which was a major industry in New York City for seven decades.

My mother also worked in the garment industry, even though she had completed two of the required three years at the teachers training school. In the early 1950s, she took and passed the civil service test and became an admissions clerk at Metropolitan Hospital on Roosevelt Island. She was thrilled when they built the new Metropolitan Hospital on First Avenue and 96th Street. She worked for the Department of Hospitals until she retired after twenty-three years.

My father was always concerned about security for himself and his family. So when he acquired his GED by attending night school, he passed the test to become a US postal employee. He began working for the postal service in 1941 and remained employed there for thirty-four years.

A government job, especially in the US Postal Service, was a pinnacle of success for a black man. My sister's violin teacher had a PhD in music, and he worked in the post office. You could probably find the most highly educated black men in the nation working there. Good pay with security! For years, it was hard to beat, and my dad was never going to blow it. So when I told him in December 1968 that I was leaving the US Weather Bureau, he exclaimed, "What? You're leaving that security!" I thought he was going to have a stroke, he was so beside himself.

After calming him down, I told him that he and mom, by providing me the opportunity to obtain an excellent education, gave me the most significant tools one needed to become secure in life. My navy career was proof of that. I was working on a master's degree that would give me even more tools to work with. I advised him to relax and watch me make it happen.

The job description for my technical specialist position in the facilities section called for me to work with the engineers and other technicians, performing site surveys for the installation of meteorological instrumentation. Those installations could be on airport runways, on lighthouses, on or within buildings, or in the middle of nowhere.

For the first couple of months, I did none of those things. My biggest and most significant assignment was to organize the facilities section's file system, which was a mess. I organized those files better than they had ever been. I was not going to give Jim McCloy any excuse to negatively say "I told you so!" regarding my selection for the position.

Eleanor Waymer, the section's administrative assistant, and Carl Caterino, the construction and maintenance representative supervisor, were aware of my dissatisfaction with how I was being used. I finally decided it was time to revolt. I went into Jim's office and presented him an ultimatum. Unless he assigned me work that fit my job description, I would sit in my office and do my homework. I would no longer perform his menial projects. I returned to my desk and opened a book.

Carl found out what took place and spoke to Silvio, the regional director, who called me into his office. I explained my situation and said that I wanted to perform the work that my job description required. I said the bureau was wasting my talent and experience and that was unfair to me and the engineering branch. Silvio made it clear he didn't want to lose me. I made it clear that whatever resulted from our meeting, I would leave the Weather

Bureau when it was advantageous to me. Until that occurred, I would do my best to excel in my job.

Jim, after a meeting with Silvio, called me into his office and proclaimed, "Wayne, I got a big assignment for you!" It was the first of many. I traveled to Maine, Massachusetts, New Hampshire, Rhode Island, Ohio, West Virginia, and North and South Carolina. The construction and maintenance representatives raved about the accuracy and detail of my surveys. I even took my son and my nephew, Donald, on a few assignments to nearby states. During the two years following my meeting with Silvio, I searched for a job in private industry.

In 1968, one of my closest friends, Barbara Harris, urged me to apply for a sales position at Johnson Publishing Company Inc., publisher of *Ebony* and *Jet* magazines. She thought that with my insurance sales experience, the position would be ideal for me. I applied and was interviewed and hired for the job by the executive vice president, William P. Grayson.

Before submitting my letter of resignation to Jim McCloy, I became euphoric. I was about to embark on an exciting new adventure, where my success would largely be determined by my perseverance, creativity, and determination. I couldn't wait to get started.

Lessons Learned Along the Way
23. An influential advocate is a great asset and worth cultivating.
24. When trying something new, test it first.
25. You can't advance in life unless you're willing to take reasonable risks.

Ebony and *Jet*

I started my first day of work at Johnson Publishing on the first working day of 1969, and I started it wrong. I was late! I hadn't used the subway regularly in more than ten years, and I neglected to allow enough time for slowdowns and delays, in addition to switching between train lines. The first thing I did upon arrival was apologize to Bill Grayson, promising him that it would never happen again. He wasn't pleased, but he accepted my apology. It never happened again.

After accompanying advertising managers and advertising representatives on several sales calls, and after studying my product, market, and sales tools, I focused on my client list. It did not have many active advertisers, but after I researched the overall market activity of the entire list, I determined it had potential for growth.

Advertising salesmen (there were no female salespeople on staff) were paid a salary plus a per page bonus for exceeding the monthly sales quota of four pages. Those who sold advertising, including managers, were spread across the country, including ten based in New York, six in Chicago, and two in Los Angeles. In 1969, my initial year, I achieved quota six out of seven months (the first issue that I could sell was April 1969). In my second year, I increased my sales 35 percent, exceeding quota ten of twelve months. In my third and final year, 1971, I increased my sales 70 percent and was named "Ebony Salesman of the Year." 1971 was the first year *Ebony* achieved $10 million in advertising sales. I sold $1 million dollars of it.

I had many accomplishments at *Ebony* magazine. One of my first was expanding the Posner Beauty Products account. The company had recently acquired a new executive vice president named Carl. Mr. Posner, the owner, had curtailed his involvement in marketing the Posner brand. Posner was angry with Johnson Publishing because Mr. Johnson was advertising his

Fashion Fair Cosmetics brand in *Ebony* without cost, which left Posner competing at a disadvantage.

I met with Carl and asked him, "What will it take to get Posner to run twelve full-color pages in *Ebony*?" Posner was currently running one full-page ad and eleven one-inch ads that allowed Posner to maintain a twelve-time rate, our lowest, for his one full-page, four-color ad. Carl presented me with his demands, which included a couple of covers, and I promised I would work on it and get back to him.

I took the request to Bill Grayson. Because the enmity between *Ebony* and Posner was so strong and covers were scarce, he told me I needed to speak with Mr. Johnson, which I did. My discussion with Mr. Johnson was direct. I stated what a twelve-time, four-color, full-page schedule, including three covers, would amount to in ad revenue and compared it with what Posner was spending. I then asked Johnson, "Do you want an additional $135,000-plus in ad revenue?

My instincts told me he couldn't turn that kind of money down, especially when he knew Posner had a legitimate gripe. No advertising representative had ever come to him with this kind of proposal from Posner before. Our own vice president for advertising, Howard Smith, disliked Mr. Posner and allowed his prejudices to get in the way of trying to do business with him. Mr. Johnson, however, was not confused. He answered, "Yes. Go get the contract."

I told Carl what I had obtained for him, and he was surprised. He didn't believe I could deliver what he asked for. I then told him that because of my successful action on his behalf, he should do something for me. I asked him to give me an order for a full-page ad for the Ebony Fashion Fair magazine, which was given to everyone who attended the Ebony Fashion Fair. The show toured the US six or seven months of the year and was attended by at least 40,000 people. Although Carl grumbled as he acceded to my request, he couldn't hide the fact that he was pleased with the deal. I was the envy of the sales staff when I returned with those contracts.

I believed I was a good salesman, but I had no problem teaming up with another entity or person to break a new account. I did so, notably, to acquire the US Navy account, which did not use paid advertising, and the Chanel account. Neither account advertised in black media.

When I began to pursue the US Navy account, donated public service ads made up the navy's entire recruitment budget. The navy did not pay for its ads. Officials wanted to recruit black officer prospects but didn't want to pay to do so. They believed that if US Navy was to buy black media, the white, southern-based companies that sponsored their ad budget might resent it and curtail their sponsorship.

There were two black naval officers who were instrumental in my effort to get the US Navy to advertise in *Ebony* and ultimately, other black media, including *Black Enterprise*. The first was Lieutenant Commander Robert L. Toney. He retired as a rear admiral after a distinguished thirty-four-year naval career. He died on November 4, 2016, and a notable statement in his obituary was the following:

> One of RADM [Rear Admiral] Toney's many significant achievements in life came during the late 1960s, when he was on a tour of duty in Washington, DC, and spearheaded a program to place more minorities into the commissioned officer ranks.

The second was Lieutenant Terry Ivory, who left the navy and had a successful career in advertising.

The major obstacle to breaking the navy account was convincing the powers that be that they could not use the same generic advertising approach they were using to attract white recruits to attract black recruits. The navy's image among its black target audience—college-educated, career-focused young men—was tarnished. I had to do something dramatic to make them see the light and spend real money to reach their market.

I spoke with Ray League, president of an up-and-coming black advertising firm, Zebra Advertising Agency, and invited him to participate with me in a joint presentation on "Why Black Media?" to the US Navy Recruitment Department staff in Washington, DC. He would present from the agency creative perspective, and I would present from the marketing and media perspective. He was all for it!

We knew each other's pitches so well that we didn't even rehearse. We went to DC and made our presentation, and we kicked ass and took names. When we departed, the powers that be realized that if they were serious about recruiting black officer material, they needed to follow our advice and pay to advertise in our media just like the US Army had been doing for years. We were not going to do it for free.

Without support from Lieutenant Commander Toney and Lieutenant Ivory, our efforts might not have succeeded. But the navy officials deserved credit. They assigned committed and dedicated black officers to fill that minority recruitment billet. The navy demonstrated that it was serious about achieving its objective. The campaign to recruit black and other minority officer prospects was a great success.

Chanel was a different story. In my only contact with the client, the vice president for marketing made it clear that everything having to do with advertising went through his agency. He would not discuss ads with me. The problem was that the account supervisor at the agency didn't want to give the time of day to black media representatives. She wouldn't take my calls or return my messages. So I called the vice president for marketing during the lunch hour when I thought his secretary would be out and he might have to answer the phone himself, and he did.

Before he could brush me off, I said to him, "You're paying a lot of money to your agency to select the right media in which to market your product. They are not serving you well if your account supervisor won't take media reps' calls or return their messages. You directed me to contact your agency, and they ignore me. Is that what they are supposed to do? I just thought you ought to be aware that you are not getting what you're paying for." He said that he would look into it.

In less than three minutes, my phone was ringing. The agency's account supervisor for Chanel was calling. "What is this I hear you can't meet with me?" she said, feigning incredulity. "Of course you can! When would you like to come in?" We set a date, and I began to plan my attack, which I knew had to be spectacular because I would only get one chance. She was seeing me under duress, so I had to overcome her anger and disdain if I was to have any chance of breaking this account. I called in Audrey Smaltz, the Ebony Fashion Fair commentator.

Audrey had recently joined *Ebony*. I had known her for almost twenty years. She was into fashion early on and modeled in fashion shows of young black designers, including John and Sylvester Weston, whose mother and mine were childhood friends. She had been featured on New York transit ads and other venues. Audrey was on her way to becoming the backstage legend she is today. She was then, as she is now, smart, sassy, and super professional. I asked her to accompany me to the Chanel meeting and to sprinkle her "fashion magic dust" on our account supervisor target.

I prepared an album of *Ebony*'s fashion advertisers and editorials to establish that the magazine's environment was highly conducive for a prime product like Chanel. I presented the account supervisor a promotional piece that stated that the black consumer was the fashion innovator of our time. Audrey was the coup de grace with her fashion knowledge. We left that Chanel account supervisor in a state of wonder. A few days later, after I had sent her my follow-up thank-you letter, the order came in.

Chanel's print campaign was limited to fashion and upscale magazines. It was not big monetarily, but it was a prestigious account. Chanel's appearance in *Ebony* was a statement to the advertising world that the magazine was a powerful advertising vehicle that should be considered for any major media buy. Chanel's presence in *Ebony* also became a significant selling point for our sales force.

Lessons Learned Along the Way

26. A strong team is an asset. Don't be reluctant to ask a teammate for assistance.

27. If you need to use a bat to get someone's attention, wrap it in cotton first.

Yvonne Cecile (Barrett) Sobers

I broke and expanded many other accounts at Johnson Publishing, but the biggest and most significant acquisition of my life was my wife, Yvonne, whom I met and married during my first year at the company. She is my greatest blessing! I believe our marriage was orchestrated by God. He blessed me with a second angel in my life because of the care and devotion I gave to Audrey, the first angel in my life.

Before I left the US Weather Bureau, and Barbara Harris was still working at Johnson Publishing, she planned to have a party in October 1968. She intended to introduce me to Yvonne, but she got sick and had to cancel the party.

When I began working at Johnson Publishing, Yvonne was the secretary to advertising manager Bill Santos and advertising representative Claude Hall. Our work area was open, and only the managers had small partitioned desk areas in the rear of the space. The eastern advertising manager, Howard Smith, also had a partitioned area on the left side, separated from the open area by the aisle that traversed the space from front to back. Privacy was nonexistent, but the openness allowed me to see and admire Yvonne every time she walked by me to consult with her bosses. My admiration increased each time she passed by.

I invited Yvonne and Joyce Thurston, our production manager, to my thirty-second birthday party that February. Yvonne had her long hair in a bouffant style. When she made her grand entrance downstairs to my basement family room, her hair almost got knocked aside when it hit the low ceiling above the staircase. My best friend, Ben Jones, asked her for her telephone number.

The breakthrough in our relationship occurred in April 1969, about fourteen weeks into my tenure at Johnson Publishing. I arrived at work shortly after 8:30 a.m. and entered through the mail room, where Yvonne and a few other employees were gathered. She was not looking pleased. She had cut her hair, and those in her company had evidently voiced their disappointment. One of them called out to me, "Look, Yvonne cut her hair!" I gave her a once over, paused, and said, "It looks nice!" She was so pleased with my response that she reached out and hugged and kissed me! From that point on, I was hooked.

I proposed marriage to her on her twenty-seventh birthday, June 3, 1969, at the fountain in front of the Plaza Hotel in New York City. We were married on August 23, 1969, in St. George's Episcopal Church in the Williamsbridge section of the Bronx. In one fell swoop, Yvonne got a house, a car, a kid, and my enduring commitment to love and cherish her forever.

We honeymooned on Cape Cod. We thought about taking Loren with us, but my sister said, "Oh, no. I will keep him with me until you get back and get settled." The unbridled love and support Yvonne and I have received from our families and close friends cannot be overstated. It remains that way, and we have never taken that love and support for granted or failed to reciprocate whenever possible.

Loren was pleased with his new mommy. When we told him in the winter of 1971 that Yvonne was going to have a baby, he told us, "I want a baby brother born on July 4!" Although it had looked doubtful, Julian Christopher Sobers arrived two weeks late on July 4, 1971.

On that day, we were supposed to go to my cousin Stephan's house in Freeport, Long Island, to celebrate the day with the Sobers family. It was customary for one of the Sobers to host a July 4 family picnic. Because Yvonne was overdue to give birth to Julian, we stayed home. My parents and Loren were picked up by my aunt Gertrude and uncle Jimmy, and they went to the picnic. As they were about to drive off, Aunt Gertrude said to Loren, "It looks like you're not going to get your wish Loren." He responded, "Is today July 4?" When she answered yes, he said, "You'll see, you'll see!"

Shortly after noon when they left, Yvonne went into labor, and I took her to Albert Einstein Medical College Hospital, where she gave birth. Once I viewed him and ascertained that Yvonne was doing fine, I called the family in Freeport to give them the good news. When someone answered the phone, I asked to speak to Loren, because I felt it would be most appropriate for him to be the first to know, given his wish and prediction. When I told him, "You have a baby brother," he dropped the phone and ran off screaming, "I got a baby brother…I got a baby brother…I got a baby brother!"

All the women wanted to get the details of the birth and were relieved that Loren hadn't hung up the phone. After I filled them in, I went back to spend time with Yvonne and admire our newborn son.

WAYNE AND YVONNE SOBERS, AUGUST 23, 1969

We went on to have Stephanie Cecile Sobers, born on "Tax Day," April 15, 1974. We raised all our children in the same manner. Yvonne, having been adopted at birth by a wonderful family, only knew an unselfish loving family life growing up. She disdained the prefix "step-" and its predominately negative image—that is, stepmother, stepfather, stepbrother, or stepsister. When Loren was fourteen, with his approval, Yvonne formally adopted him. We became one family without distinctions.

Lesson Learned Along the Way

28. Cherish the love and support you receive from others. Reciprocate it, and do not take it for granted.

Black Enterprise: The Invitation

Jeanette Ford was an advertising assistant who worked at Johnson Publishing with Yvonne and me. Before that, she had worked with Earl Graves when he was an aide to Senator Robert Kennedy. After Kennedy's assassination, Earl formed the Earl G. Graves Publishing Co. Inc., and in August 1970, published the first edition of *Black Enterprise* magazine. The magazine was an instant success and was profitable after its tenth issue.

Earl contacted Jeanette and asked her who was the best salesman at *Ebony* magazine. She gave him my name, Earl called me, and we met and discussed our hopes and desires. He asked me to join him at *Black Enterprise*. I told him I would consider his offer.

My reputation as a "very good and professional salesman" in the New York advertising sales community was growing. I had recently turned down an offer to be *Newsweek*'s "black" salesman. The salary they offered me I had already achieved at Johnson Publishing, and I told that to the interviewer, the advertising director. During the interview, I mentioned that it was likely that he would move up the ladder at *Newsweek*, and I asked, "What's the likelihood for me to get your job if that happens?" I don't remember his exact response, but he was not pleased with my audacity.

After considering Earl's invitation to join his company, I declined for several reasons. The primary reason was that I had just begun my final year of study for my MBA, and I didn't believe I could manage both school and the workload that a fledgling magazine required (*Black Enterprise* had just published its third issue). The other reason was that although I had achieved much in my career in a short time, I believed I needed to catch my breath. I just wasn't ready.

I mentioned my meeting with Earl to my boss, Bill Grayson. I told him that I believed I was not being paid commensurate with my performance, and I requested that it be rectified. I also stated that I had received offers from other entities and that I might leave Johnson Publishing. I concluded telling him that if I accepted an offer elsewhere, Johnson Publishing "would not be able to buy me back."

The next October, Earl called me again. This time my personal situation was much more favorable. I had completed my coursework for my MBA and was working on my thesis. Yvonne had given birth to Julian that year. My vision was clear. Johnson Publishing had not improved my compensation package, even though I was on my way to achieving an *Ebony* sales record of more than $1 million in advertising sales.

This time, our conversation about me joining *Black Enterprise* was simple. The magazine had just published its thirteenth issue, and I was ready for the challenge. We shook hands on the fundamentals of our deal on the southeast corner of Madison Avenue and 41st Street in New York City. All that remained was to notify Bill Grayson that I was leaving Johnson Publishing.

When I gave Bill Grayson my letter of resignation, he shook his head. I thanked him for recognizing my potential and for providing me the opportunity to enter the business world. He wasn't happy at losing his "million-dollar man." Shortly thereafter, I received a call from John H. Johnson, who was not accustomed to losing any employee he really wanted to keep and did not ever welcome anyone back who ever quit.

He opened the call with, "Mr. Sobers! What's this I hear about you leaving? I thought you were married to JPC!" He went on to say that he had been preoccupied getting the corporate headquarters building, under construction in the heart of the Chicago's Loop, on South Michigan Avenue, completed. No other black-owned business in the nation owned its own building in a major city's downtown business district. It was a bona fide accomplishment of which he was justly proud. He told me I would be promoted to associated advertising manager with a salary increase. I listened and asked if I could have a day to think it over. He said yes.

I did not want to be abrupt or rude to Mr. Johnson. I had too much respect for him and what he had achieved. I was proud to work for Johnson Publishing and recognized that he had given me a chance to succeed based on merit with no hidden agendas. But I had committed myself to Earl, and nothing Mr. Johnson was likely to offer was going to change my decision. My commitment to helping Earl Graves build a business whose objective was to spearhead the growth of black entrepreneurship was cast in stone.

The next day, I called Mr. Johnson and politely declined his offer. He told me if things did not work out for me in the future and I wanted to make a change, he should be the first person I contact. Bill Grayson later told me that Mr. Johnson frequently referred to me as "the one that got away." I began my fifteen-and-a-half-year adventure at *Black Enterprise* on November 1, 1971.

Lesson Learned Along the Way
29. Don't burn your bridges behind you. You may need to cross them again.

Black Enterprise: Accepting the Challenge

I began my career at *Black Enterprise* as it was about to publish its January 1972 issue. My years there would be filled with unbounded opportunity and all types of challenges, most of which enhanced my growth as a business and financial executive, a media professional, and a leader.

My initial title was manager of marketing services. We had a dedicated and outstanding staff headed by Earl G. Graves, publisher. Other notable members were Pat Patterson, editor; Edward L. Towles, art director; Jim Bell, director of advertising; Esther Craig, controller; and Robert Graves, assistant circulation manager. There was a great comradery throughout the staff. Everyone knew they were a key to the magazine's success, and not one employee was treated as an afterthought.

The magazine's board of advisers comprised Senator Edward Brooke; Earl G. Graves; Representative John Lewis, who was then director of the Voter Education Project; William Hudgins, vice chairman of the board of directors of the Freedom National Bank; Julian Bond, then a Georgia state representative; Congresswoman Shirley Chisolm; Thomas A. Johnson, a *New York Times* staff writer; Henry Parks, president of H. G. Parks; and Mayor Charles Evers of Fayette, Mississippi.

The board members were high-profile, influential people who "felt the health—indeed the survival—of this nation would depend upon the extent to which our ethnic minorities could participate in and profit from our economic system." In those early years, members of the board, especially John Lewis and Julian Bond, helped us get meetings with many of the nation's top executives. We made it clear that we wanted them to become advertisers in *Black Enterprise* because it would be a profitable marketing opportunity for them. We knew if they advertised for "feel good" reasons as opposed to marketing reasons, that their time in the magazine would be short lived. We planned to be around for a long time.

I jumped into my new job with too much gusto. I tried to do everything to make a difference, as if my being at the magazine was supposed to make and immediate and obvious impact, which was impossible. I didn't get enough rest, and a few days before Christmas, I was worn out.

Preparing at home for our family Christmas celebration, I was sweeping dust in the family room, and I inhaled some of it and I knew I was going to be sick. I asked Yvonne if she had any errands that were crucial for me to complete, to let me do them right away because "I will surely be sick tomorrow." The next day, Christmas, I had a fever and chills and felt awful. Our guests came, and all I could do was sit bundled up in a chair in our den staring at a television. I couldn't even eat dinner.

Lesson Learned Along the Way
30. Plan your work meticulously and pace yourself accordingly. "Rome was not built in a day."

Black Enterprise: 1971–80

My primary responsibility was to bring new advertisers on board and service and expand the accounts of our current advertisers. Jim Bell, director of advertising, and I developed a great working and personal relationship. We had many successes in my first year. In June 1973, we inaugurated the "Black Enterprise 100" issue, the definitive listing of the nation's leading black-owned businesses.

Among my early account acquisitions were New York Life, the Bermuda Department of Tourism, Saab-Scania of America Inc., John Deere, and the US Navy. These accounts readily come to mind primarily because of the unique methods and actions I incorporated into my sales approach to get them to change their minds and decide that *Black Enterprise* would work for them.

New York Life was a classic example of how a personal and professional accomplishment made a headstrong executive, with a less-than-neutral opinion of *Black Enterprise*, pay attention to my advertising presentation. Gus S., vice president for marketing and a former US Marine pilot whose military bearing was still evident in his personality and movement, finally acquiesced to see me after many requests for a meeting. Through my initial telephone contact and "scuttlebutt," I had ascertained that he viewed *Black Enterprise* as a civil rights and affirmative action buy, not a solid marketing opportunity. He advertised in *Ebony*, so he felt that he was doing his "black thing" and that was sufficient.

When I entered his office, he greeted me with low enthusiasm. I spotted a picture of an aircraft carrier on one of his walls. I walked over to view it up close and recognized that it was an operational photo of the USS Constellation. I asked Gus if he had served on it. Before answering yes, he asked me, "How did you know it's the Constellation?" I gave him a synopsis of my naval career, and everything from that point on was smooth sailing. We became comrades in arms, and I had his full attention and respect. New York Life became a regular six-time advertiser for many years.

For the Bermuda Department of Tourism account, I had to find young families for their advertising agency to use in their ads after I had convinced key client operatives that *Black Enterprise* was loaded with readers who fit their target demographic. Our prospects just happened to be black. Finding young, sophisticated black families to take a free trip to Bermuda was easy. I offered the opportunity to one associate and two close friends who fit the bill.

John Deere was one of those moments when I needed to do the obvious: make a telephone call. We were in an editorial meeting discussing a special issue, "The Business of Farming." The cover featured a prominent black farmer sitting on a John Deere tractor. I found John Deere's director of advertising and called him. I explained the opportunity to maximize his product's placement on the cover of a prominent national magazine, that it would be seen by a burgeoning untapped market in an exclusive positive editorial environment. It was an offer he couldn't refuse, and it was a breakthrough for *Black Enterprise*.

Saab-Scania of America Inc., took a lot of preparation, research, and patience. A prominent ally in my quest to acquire this account was the company's regional service manager, Will South, a subscriber to *Black Enterprise*. He worked out of Saab's eastern regional headquarters in Orange, Connecticut.

He called on me one day and offered me the opportunity to drive a Saab Turbo for a week. He told me that other general market publications had received similar opportunities, but this was the first time he offered it to a medium directed to the black consumer that matched the Saab target demographic. I accepted the offer, and by week's end, I was in love with the car, as was my father, Yvonne, and everyone else who rode in it. This was an automobile that should have been advertising in *Black Enterprise*, and I was determined to make it happen.

I wanted to buy a Saab, but I would not purchase any product of a non–*Black Enterprise* advertiser if a product in the same category was advertised in the magazine. All else equal, an advertiser's product would take preference. If I wanted to purchase a Saab, I would have to get them to advertise.

By the time a presentation was scheduled with the Saab advertising director, I was prepared. I anticipated that he would be reluctant to advertise in *Black Enterprise*, so I analyzed their advertising schedule, expenditures, and the schedules' readership duplication. I then devised a plan that illustrated what magazines, and pages therein, he could eliminate and replace with a twelve-time schedule in *Black Enterprise*.

As soon as I sat down in the ad director's office, he began a soliloquy about why he could not advertise in *Black Enterprise*. I listened without saying a word, and when he finished, he looked at me as if he expected me to get up and leave. Instead I said, "I agree with every word you said." He was surprised by my statement. I said, "Let me show you a way you can advertise in *Black Enterprise* without requiring any additional funds for your ad budget."

I laid my plan on him with a flourish. The plan highlighted his current "duplication" numbers and demonstrated cuts he could make in his current schedule without losing any readership. He could then use the cost savings to add *Black Enterprise* to his schedule and reach a new market that fit his demographic target. The benefit to Saab was that it would effectively and empathetically reach black consumers, which he wasn't doing with the campaign he had.

The advertising director agreed with my premise with minimal reluctance. He promised to study it further, and we would talk some more. In reality, he had to find a way to do it without being attacked by potential detractors and other publications that also coveted his advertising. I departed, urging him, in jest, not to take too long because he would be delaying me from buying a Saab.

A few months later, he called and said he was adding *Black Enterprise* and a women's magazine to the Saab advertising schedule. The women's magazine was his cover and, as he admitted to me, a guise for his special market campaign. So my efforts got the women's magazine some ad pages for several years. All that took place so he could have an acceptable reason for advertising in *Black Enterprise*. All I cared was that I legitimately got the business, and that was fine with me.

The US Navy was easy because I had already broken the account when I was at *Ebony*, and my efforts led to them instituting a budget to pay for advertising, at least in minority publications. Most of the key operatives were still in place, and *Black Enterprise* was a stellar medium for the account. Soon after joining the magazine, I went hard after the account and acquired it.

In an advertising and editorial meeting in March 1987, we focused on maximizing our advertising revenue for our flagship issue, the June 1987 "Black Enterprise 100." In attendance were key sales, public relations, editorial, and production people. We discussed who among our advertising prospects and editorial subjects might be able to do more or were "missing in action." Earl Graves thought that Johnson Publishing was one such company and wondered how we could make it happen. I gave it a little thought and chimed in, "That's easy. Put Mr. Johnson on the cover. He deserves it!" It wasn't difficult to reach that conclusion. His company was the number-one black-owned business listed in the issue. Johnson was a stalwart in the publishing industry. Johnson Publishing owned and operated eight businesses and divisions, three of which were media companies, and no other media had ever featured him as we would. I thought he would be flattered by the recognition. It was a no-brainer.

Everybody thought it was a great suggestion. Earl went to his office to call Mr. Johnson. He returned after about fifteen minutes saying that Mr. Johnson was "almost moved to tears with the honor." It was said that, in the past, he had turned down a cover opportunity on *Time* magazine because they frequently used caricatures of subjects on their covers and he didn't trust them to do a caricature of him.

John H. Johnson graced the June 1987 cover of *Black Enterprise* magazine's "Top 100 Black Businesses" issue and was named the "Entrepreneur of the Decade." Johnson Publishing ran ten four-color, full-page product and corporate ads. In addition, the Chrysler Corporation, citing Mr. Johnson as the newest member of its board of directors, ran an extra page saluting his designation as "Entrepreneur of the Decade." The ad revenue we gained from this highly deserved editorial recognition of Mr. Johnson exceeded $100,000.

On the "publisher's page" of that issue, Earl announced that I would be leaving the magazine after fifteen and a half years. I was going attend the General Motors Dealer Development Academy to learn how to own and operate my own automobile dealership.

Lessons Learned Along the Way
31. You should be ready to go the extra mile to accomplish your task and achieve your goal.
32. You can't get the business if you don't clearly ask for the order.
33. Look for opportunities that facilitate connecting and empathizing with the people you interact with. It can open doors for you.

STATION: CHAPPAQUA

The 1970s were full of business and life events, most of them good but some of them not.

My fifteen and a half years at Earl G. Graves Ltd. was a period of consistent growth, personally and professionally. I pioneered several new company positions, was instrumental in acquiring and overseeing three subsidiaries, and led and developed two national organizations that fostered the growth and influence of minority media.

Jim Bell and I were a potent advertising and marketing team, and I was sad when he left the company in 1973. Upon his departure, I was promoted to vice president for advertising and marketing. During the next three years, *Black Enterprise* equaled or exceeded its sales goals.

I built an extraordinary advertising sales team that was diverse in gender and race, opened a Chicago sales office, and added an advertising representative firm to solicit business for *Black Enterprise* on the West Coast. I promoted Patsy Jennings, our marketing services coordinator, to become Earl G. Graves Publishing Company's first female advertising account executive. She left *Black Enterprise* in 1975 and began a twenty-five-year advertising sales career at the *New York Times*, which she culminated as the managing director of classified advertising. That same year, I was named senior vice president of our parent company, Earl G. Graves Ltd.

In 1973, I was involved in the organizational and business aspects of my church, St. Luke's Episcopal Church in the Bronx. As the warden and building chairman, I directed a two-year marketing effort to raise $160,000 to expand the church. I cultivated the support and influence of Bishop Moore, bishop of the Episcopal Diocese of New York, and his suffragan, Bishop Wetmore, who was instrumental in opening the right doors for me and my committee.

Yvonne and I decided to move to an area that offered an excellent school system for our children. We set our sights on Westchester County. Yvonne was pregnant with Stephanie, and I searched for housing in spring 1974, ultimately focusing on Chappaqua, which was known for its outstanding school system. It was also a good commute to the heart of the New York City, which was important to me. Chappaqua was served by the Harlem Line, and its station was thirty-two miles north of Grand Central Terminal, the line's New York City terminus. Our office was one block from the terminal's entrance.

We moved into our new home in September 1974. It was on a cul-de-sac, situated on a one-and-a-quarter-acre plot with plenty of grass and trees. It had four bedrooms, two and a half bathrooms, a dining room, an eat-in kitchen, a living room, a family room, a den, a two-car garage, and an attic the length and width of the entire house. It represented the fulfillment of another one of my dreams, and the entire family loved it.

E.G.G. Dallas Broadcasting Inc.

Black Enterprise was growing in readership, influence, stature, and profitability, and Earl G. Graves Ltd., was ready to expand. Stanley Kaplan, one of Earl's associates from when he was one of Senator Robert Kennedy's top aides, owned an FM radio station in Charlotte, North Carolina. He urged Earl to consider purchasing a radio station, and Earl favored the suggestion.

Robert Tate joined *Black Enterprise* as director of advertising in summer 1976, which allowed me to assume overall responsibility for operation and financial planning of all the firm's affiliates that fall. Stanley Kaplan felt I could oversee a broadcast operation, and he volunteered to train me in the radio broadcasting business.

I attended several American Management Association training seminars and courses on the broadcasting business, including the nuances of buying a broadcast property. I spent a week at Stanley's radio station in Charlotte, learning the day-to-day aspects of the business.

We set basic parameters for a property to be considered for purchase: The property had to be in a major market, have strong potential for growth, and be readily accessible, daily, by air transportation.

The station we purchased, KNOK AM and FM in Dallas–Fort Worth, Texas, met our criteria. But the station's FM signal needed to be strengthened.

The station was in north Fort Worth, and its signal was weak over south Dallas, where much of that city's black population, our primary target audience, lived. Our consulting engineer, William (Bill) Carr, assured us we could relocate our antenna and transmitter to another tower that would be higher and closer to Dallas, increasing our coverage. The AM facility's operation was a "daytimer," limited to broadcasting between sunrise and sunset.

The major financing source for the stations was a loan from the Equitable Life Insurance Co. Inc., and a small equity investment came from Equico Capital Corp., the Equitable Minority Enterprise Small Business Investment Corporation. The total from both sources amounted to 110 percent of our purchase price. I handled all the negotiations for the purchase, accompanied by our attorneys. The legal fees were onerous. The Equitable used one of New York City's major law firms to handle its part of the deal, and Equico's law firm was that of the late Reginald F. Lewis. His conflict with Earl Graves over his legal fee pertaining to our deal is partially chronicled in his autobiography, *Why Should White Guys Have All the Fun? How Reginald Lewis Created a Billion-Dollar Business Empire.*

The conflict arose because Earl thought Reggie's legal fees were too high, which was not an unusual complaint. My task was to get the fee reduced. I met with Reggie in his Broad Street office. I wasn't making any progress, so I suggested that he and Earl meet to discuss it further. Because neither was personally acquainted with the other, I thought it would be mutually beneficial.

The meeting took place at our office on Madison Avenue. It was a cordial and open meeting. Reggie articulated the extent of the work his firm performed to justify his fee. After the meeting ended, Earl concluded that Reggie's firm probably did more work on the deal than the Equitable's law firm. The major dispute arose when Reggie demanded his fee be paid at closing. Earl said he would pay the bill in 30 days, which Reggie said was "unacceptable," and declared, "If we don't get it, we're not closing."

Earl called the Equitable chairman and CEO, Coy Eklund, to complain about Reggie. Reggie relented after the Equitable assured him he would receive his fee on time. No hard feelings resulted between Earl and Reggie from that encounter.

At the radio station's closing in October 1977, Earl slid the million-dollar check over for my signature. I deferred to him, saying that I thought that his name should be on that check. Earl's gesture was an affirmation of his trust and respect for my integrity and competence.

We introduced William (Bill) Chatman to the staff as their new vice president and general manager. "Sis" Kaplan, Stanley's wife, along with the former owner, were on hand to assist Bill and me with transitioning the operation to E.G.G. Dallas Broadcasting.

I returned to New York to attend my first Equitable Variable Life Insurance Company (EVLICO) board of directors meeting. But over the next six months, I remained in Fort Worth for extended periods until I was satisfied that the operation was functioning as planned under our capable general manager.

As with most radio station acquisitions, the new ownership must inform the staff of the changes that will occur and forewarn them about the high standards of performance they will be expected to maintain. To be effective, that message must be delivered in a positive and reassuring manner so that the strong employees will be happy to stay and the weak or ineffective employees will realize they must either "shape up or ship out."

Most of the on-air staff were black, and most performed well. They were inspired by the new black ownership and the affiliation with *Black Enterprise*. Most of the support staff were white female Texans and were nervous about working for black ownership. Ironically, Sis Kaplan, a white woman, upset them to no end!

Sis was knowledgeable about operating a radio station, and she tried to change everything all at once, which upset and confused the support staff. Sis knew what she wanted, but she did not have the patience or personality to convey her know-how. I stepped in and curtailed her "attack" to salvage those among the staff who were worth salvaging.

The three people under assault by Sis were Mary Ann John, Geneva Ladner, and a "Ms. Q." I took Sis aside, and we prioritized the changes we needed to make to get her system up and running. Then, I got the ladies together, with Sis in the background, and we outlined the steps to get the job done. The ladies realized that I had recognized their plight. I relieved them of the unnecessary pressure being applied to them, and they calmed down, focused, and proceeded to get the job done. They developed a new positive attitude.

Shortly thereafter, Mary Ann told me she and Geneva supported the new ownership and were not going anywhere. But she thought Ms. Q was contemplating leaving and asked if I would try to get her to stay. I did speak with her, and during our discussion, she divulged that she "had a dog that didn't like black people" and that it became "vicious towards black people whenever they approached." I figured she was a lost cause, and I didn't press her to stay. She soon quit.

Sis Kaplan was helpful during our acquisition, but she presented a problem for me. She perceived her role as Earl's agent behind the scenes. She was his friend and loyal to him. She didn't know about my personal and business relationship with Earl. So when she went behind my back and called Earl about something she thought I did, I had to confront him.

During the transition, Sis had suggested to Earl and me that we not bestow the title of "program director" on anyone until later, when we could better evaluate our broadcasting staff's talent. I agreed, but someone had to be responsible for that department's basic functions. Neither I nor Bill Chatman could perform those functions and carry out our responsibilities at the same time, so we delegated that function to Dwayne Dancer. The delegated tasks were among those that a program director would perform, but we did not give Dwayne the title or imply that he would become that person.

When Sis thought I had promoted Dwayne, not realizing what we had really done, she told Earl. Earl called me, with Stanley Kaplan conferenced in, questioning me about what Sis said.

Stanley said, "I thought we had an agreement not to appoint anyone to be program director at this time." I responded curtly, "That's correct." "Then, why did you make Dwayne the program director?" he asked. I said, "I didn't. Who said I did?" I told them what I had done and concluded with, "Do you have any more questions?" They paused, and I hung up.

A few days later, Earl came down to Texas. We were going to call on the Dallas mayor. As Earl and I drove to Dallas City Hall, I told him that what Sis did was underhanded and disrespectful, and I thought he should have told her that she should have discussed the matter with me before she called him.

Part of our purchasing agreement was that we would keep the former general manager, Stu Hepburn, on as a consultant. But his presence was detrimental to the positive environment we were creating, so we asked him to leave, paid him off, and wished him well.

Our meetings with the market's influencers and opinion makers, in conjunction with our promotion activities, began to show positive results. KNOK-FM was becoming a formidable competitor, not only to KLRD, the other black-oriented FM station in Dallas whose morning drive-time star was Tom Joyner, but in the entire market as well. Our nickname was the "The Black Rocker," and our logo was an image of a Bentwood rocking chair. We gave Bentwood rocking chairs to the mayors of Dallas and Fort Worth and a few other notables in our market.

We purchased and remodeled an RV into a mobile radio station, which we used for remote broadcasts all around the Dallas–Fort Worth metroplex. We also changed the call letters of KNOK-AM to KDJZ, on which we implemented an all-jazz format. It was well accepted, but its effectiveness was muted because the station was only licensed for daytime operation, which was not the best time for broadcasting jazz. But it was better than simulcasting the FM programing, and it provided us a unique product to market.

On Sunday mornings, a religious format was broadcasted on the AM station when it was KNOK, and we continued to do so when it became KDLZ. Several years later, we would change the format to all religious and rename the station KHVN. It was another unique change in the market, and it was well received. The daytimer was like an unwanted appendage, and any revenue we could generate with it was a bonus.

The action that accounted for much of the station's early competitiveness was the hiring of a programming consultant—a "radio doctor." On Stanley Kaplan's recommendation, we hired Kent Burkhardt, whose expertise served us well until our primary weakness, our lack of a strong signal over south Dallas, began to hurt our ratings.

Several people on our advisory board thought a new general manager would be the answer to our revenue stagnation. Their assessment was not based on any direct knowledge, observation, or expertise in broadcasting. I objected to firing Bill Chatman, but they wanted someone younger and flashier to bring new energy. I told them they were making a mistake and that they would not get a person more qualified or dedicated to the getting the job done than Bill.

I had to deliver the bad news to Bill. I have had to dismiss many employees in my business career. Earl was not a confrontational person, and he sent others, usually me, to deliver bad tidings. He would say I was the only person he knew who could fire someone and have that person thank me for doing so. Nevertheless, dismissing Bill Chatman was one of the saddest tasks I have ever performed, especially because he didn't deserve it.

Stanley Kaplan came up with another prospect, Gary Lewis. Gary was brash, energetic, and polished, and he knew the business. He interviewed well. Stanley liked him, and I had no reason to think differently, so we hired him.

Gary also recruited two men he had worked with at a prior station, Jeffrey Myers and Harry Thompson, to be local sales manager and national sales manager, respectively.

Before Bill Chatman's departure, Kent Burkhardt recommended we hire a new program director to follow his system without deviation, which he identified as a flaw in the previous person who filled the position. I felt that Kent might have been getting concerned that his reputation might become shaded if KNOK didn't do better in the ratings, and that's why he wanted us to hire Kelly as our new program director.

Sometime later, when Kent was monitoring our programming, he found that Kelly occasionally deviated from his plan. When he confronted Kelly, he was told that Gary was overruling him and threatening to fire him if he didn't follow his edicts. About that time, Earl got a call from a contact in Dallas that Gary was using drugs. The source was dependable.

We flew to Fort Worth and met with Gary, Jeffrey, and Harry. After having them take a voluntary drug test, we presented them with the results. Aside from a trace of marijuana, Harry and Jeffrey were clean. Gary tested positive for cocaine and was directed to get treatment, which the company covered. All of them were warned about the consequences if they violated the rules regarding drug use.

Later in the year, a general manager on the West Coast told me he knew about Gary's previous drug use and he thought he had told me when he heard we were considering hiring him as our GM. I would never have consented to his hire, without instituting safeguards like a drug test, if I had known.

I abhor drug use. People who get hooked on drugs lose self-control, exercise poor judgement, and become their own worst enemy. I saw too many lives ruined because of drug use while I was growing up. Gary's action was disappointing, and it had a negative impact on my life at that time.

To ensure that the radio stations were functioning properly and profitably, for more than a year and a half, I spent three to five days a week in Texas. I maintained an apartment in Arlington, midway between our Fort Worth broadcast facility and headquarters and our Dallas sales office. I flew Braniff International Airways with such regularity that the boarding crew at New York's LaGuardia Airport would assign me a seat each Monday before I appeared at check in.

Before checking in for my return flight, usually on a Friday afternoon, I would go into the Baskin-Robbins ice cream shop in the airline terminal. After several months, the lady behind the counter asked if I worked at the airport. I had become a familiar sight at the Dallas–Fort Worth International Airport.

Earl asked Ben Tucker, a legendary jazz musician and former owner of WSOK in Savannah, Georgia, to temporarily run the stations after I told him I was leaving Earl G. Graves Ltd. to attend the General Motors Dealer Development Academy in April 1987.

Another reason that Earl asked Ben to fulfill the general manager role at KNOK was that we needed a programmer because Kent Burkhardt was no longer programming our stations. He and Earl had a falling out over his performance. Ben Tucker programmed his own station, WSOK, and it was the number-one station in Savannah for about thirteen years. He filled a crucial role for our company.

The stations were sold around 1989. A plan for relocating KNOK's broadcasting antenna to a new tower was developed, but it was not implemented before the sale.

Equitable Variable Life Insurance Company

Coy Eklund, chairman and CEO of the Equitable Variable Life Insurance Company, thought the world of Earl Graves, and the feeling was mutual. When EVLICO, a wholly owned subsidiary of the Equitable, wanted to add another outside director to its board, Coy extended the first invitation to Earl. But because Earl was a member of the ITT board of directors, and the Hartford Insurance Company was owned by ITT, he had to decline the invitation.

Earl suggested that if they really wanted someone on their board who knew the insurance business, they ought to consider me because I formerly owned an insurance business and was licensed in all forms of insurance. Because Coy held Earl in such high esteem, it was hard to dismiss his recommendation. I was subsequently invited to lunch with David H. Harris, chairman and CEO of EVLICO, and his chief insurance officer. The luncheon went well, and I was asked to join the board of directors. It was an honor to have been elected, and I took the appointment seriously. The first people I informed of my appointment were my parents. I telephoned them and had each of them pick up a phone so I could give them the good news at the same time. They were proud.

I learned a great deal and participated on the board as a member of the budget committee. As of October 1977, EVLICO was the only insurance company in the US offering variable life insurance to the general public. It was licensed in thirty-two states. When I left the board about six years later, the company was licensed in forty-eight states and the District of Columbia, and the company was responsible for 80 percent of the Equitable's new insurance business.

Considering how few people of African descent were on major corporate boards, my election to the EVLICO board of directors was significant. I was not famous, nor was I a brand name, so it signaled to the black business community that I was elected because EVLICO believed I could make a real contribution as a member of its board of directors and the company.

The Siding

In 1977, I became a 50 percent owner, by default, of the Siding Restaurant. It was the worst investment of my life. The experience I gained from that near disaster was phenomenal but was emotionally and financially hurtful for almost a decade.

The Siding was originally a small railroad warehouse located on a railroad siding about two hundred yards north of the Harlem Line's Chappaqua station. I don't know when it was converted into a restaurant. When it came to my attention, it was owned by a group of investors led by an entrepreneur named Curtiss Buseman.

One of my neighbors, Horace Wolfson, was the business' bookkeeper. I met him through his wife, Lorraine. Our families were both members of the Church of St. Mary the Virgin. Horace didn't attend the church because he was of a different faith.

When I met Horace, I had just started on the EVLICO board, and I anticipated having extra money to invest. I was considering building a tennis court behind our house. I was also pondering my family's future needs—for example, Loren would soon be ready to attend college. A good investment could generate extra revenue that would help defray future college expenses. Things were going well, and I was in a receptive state of mind.

Originally, I was asked to be one of four investors. Horace was another. Another was a friend of Horace's I didn't know well, and the last was the restaurant's cook. The latter two withdrew from the deal at the last minute, which should have raised a larger red flag than it did. Horace managed to convince me that he was up to the task of running the Siding, but I later learned he wasn't.

Another bad sign appeared at the closing, when I learned that Sidney Liebowitz, my lawyer for Earl G. Graves Ltd., was representing the seller,

Curtiss Buseman. Sidney and I were uncomfortable sitting across the table from one another after having worked so closely and so well together for the past six years. After the deal, Sidney resigned from representing Buseman.

My greatest shortcoming was not requesting weekly or monthly financial reports on the business' status from the accountant. He reported to Horace and didn't alert me when trouble arose. The accountant assumed Horace was keeping me abreast of the business's financial status, and as a principal owner of the company, he should have told me that Horace had fallen behind in paying the Siding's federal taxes. Before telling me, Horace went to the IRS and signed an agreement for the corporation to pay the unpaid taxes. I subsequently met with the IRS agent to ensure that I was fully informed about what had taken place and what our obligations were.

I put various safeguards in place to prevent further damage. I was furious with Horace because this could have been avoided if he had been up front about it. He couldn't deal with the fact that the Siding was underperforming financially. He was embarrassed. Once again, he was failing in one of his endeavors. I later discovered that he had also fallen behind with our New York State payroll tax. That omission would plague me for seven years.

I had to do something positive to turn the situation around quickly. I closeted myself in my office one morning and assessed my options. Giving up was not one of them. I resolved that my election to the EVLICO board of directors could be part of my salvation. I knew that the debt would fall on me because the IRS had determined that Horace was penniless. The IRS doesn't care who they get their money from, so they will go after anyone who can be legally bound to the debt.

I realized that the long-term solution to my plight was my job. As long as I continued to perform at my maximum ability, I could overcome my predicament and continue to prosper. I made that mission a priority, second only to taking care of my family.

The first step was to get on the same page with the IRS, to work with them to have an opportunity to pay them without being harassed. I met with the agent handling our account and requested that I pay half of the debt in one year and the second half in two years, assuring him that I had a plan to accomplish the full payment. I did not disclose my plan but only said that it was based on certain anticipated income: my Equitable stipend. He accepted my proposition. Why? Because, as he had told me in our first encounter, "Most businesses that make an agreement with the IRS to pay off back taxes go belly up."

I told Horace to look for buyers for the Siding. Because he didn't have any money, we had to sell the business. He couldn't even do that right. Every time we met with a potential buyer, Horace discouraged them by ranting about his "difficulty in getting good help," which was not true.

In my view, besides Horace, the restaurant had two drawbacks, both correctable. First, the facility was too large and it required more patrons than one could reasonably acquire on a regular basis, other than weekends. The second was that there was no promotional budget to attract more patrons. Promotions targeted to attract more patrons for the Tuesday-through-Thursday dinner hours would have accomplished that. Eventually, I had to shut the Siding down. The few assets that we could sell were sold. The financial burden of that fiasco was totally on me.

My lawyer, Lawrence Cohen, had filed a malpractice suit against the accountant, which we won in the lower court but lost in the court of appeals, the highest court in the State of New York. What had annoyed me most was the final verdict. The court ruled that "the corporation had to sue the accountant since that was the entity that was damaged," not me, the individual.

But then why was the IRS making me pay? The IRS part of this fiasco cost me more than $24,000.

The New York State sales and payroll tax part of the Siding disaster escalated, after several years, to more than $94,000, including interest and penalties. I fought this debt tooth and nail, and thanks to attorneys James H. Tully Jr. and Robert Plautz, I was offered a favorable deal.

Attorney Plautz uncovered a significant concern of the New York State Tax Commission that was so ominous that if the commission went to court with my case and lost, it would set a damaging precedent. The commission determined that it was a risk they wanted to avoid. My attorney told the commission we were open to an offer to settle. But he insisted that all penalties had to be waived, to which the commission agreed. The interest on the resolved amount in the settlement could not be waived.

The amount of the proposed settlement was $24,312 versus the states' suit of $94,220. I had already learned from my failed attempt to sue the Siding's accountant that I could not put my faith in receiving a favorable court decision, no matter how strong my case appeared to be. Accepting the states offer was a no-brainer. I jumped at it.

Horace had promised to repay me when he sold his house, which was not something I could bank on. He died before I settled with the state. At his funeral, which I attended, his father-in-law, who never liked him, was surprised that I was there. He asked me, "How come you're here after what Horace did to you?" I responded that "Horace might have been a bad manager, but he was not a bad person. I didn't hate him." I was there to support Lorraine, Horace's wife, and her children, who were our friends. He then said that if he were in my place, he wouldn't have come. Then he complimented me on my actions and walked away.

Earl Graves was tremendously supportive during the Siding ordeal. It was through his initiative that I acquired Tully and Plautz as my attorneys, another one of my many blessings. His help was invaluable.

BCI Marketing Inc.

One business opportunity presented to Earl G. Graves Ltd. was a newspaper coupon insert targeted to black consumers and distributed via black newspapers. It was named Black Consumer Inserts (BCI). Henry Hay, an acquaintance, was associated with the product, and he brought the owner to our office. BCI was struggling, and he wanted to sell it. We discussed the project, its potential, and its shortcomings, and we agreed to acquire it. Henry, who was experienced in the sale of black media, became the marketing director of the company we established to sell it, BCI Marketing Inc., and I became its president.

The products struggled because black newspapers' circulation figures were unreliable, and black publishers' commitment to support it was tepid. The publishers wanted the revenue that BCI would bring them, but they didn't want the additional cost that came with stuffing the insert into their newspapers. The product could not be successful if the publishers didn't deliver all our inserts, so we had to get them committed and involved.

We also had to develop marketing research data for a sales team, which we had not yet acquired, to help our sales effort. We fulfilled both tasks by contracting with two separate companies, each owned and operated by an experienced black professional executive, Thomas Dixon and Al Wellington.

Tom is an experienced retail marketing and merchandising consultant. His company at the time was Profitable Formulas Inc. Tom, using his expertise on how supermarkets support and merchandise their products, worked with Henry Hay to launch and maintain our sales efforts, which were primarily client driven as opposed to advertising agency driven. We had to call more on merchandising managers and directors and clients rather than account executives at advertising agencies. That entailed a lot of travel to consummate sales because the manufacturers are spread throughout the country while most major advertising agencies are clustered in about ten national and regional media centers.

Alan Wellington was an excellent marketing researcher. His company, the Wellington Group Inc., focused on the black consumer's shopping characteristics, for which reliable information was sparse. Most general market research treated the black consumer market as an afterthought. If a general market company elected to target that segment, it usually relied on black media to provide the data to support its position.

The research that black media provided was good, and the companies and their ad agencies usually accepted it because they had none of their own. Most companies were aware of the black consumer market and its potential but felt that what motivated white people to buy their product was the same for black people. But often, there were significant differences for why black folks chose a particular brand compared with their white counterparts.

Before the formation of Earl G. Graves Ltd., *Black Enterprise* had formed a subsidiary that produced Black Consumer Index, a major market research work that had the largest sample of black heads of household ever compiled. At the time, I was senior vice president of Earl G. Graves Ltd., and I was president of BCI Marketing Inc., charged with revitalizing the sale of the Black Consumer Index.

Al Wellington's research work could support the sales strategy we developed for Black Consumer Inserts because it was more product specific and more current. The Black Consumer Index was ten years old. Our products complemented each other and brought positive attention to both. Al usually accompanied us when we made major presentations.

Our product was good, as were our presentation and graphics, but our distribution via black newspapers, was questionable. We had to depend on the newspapers to stuff the inserts. Redemption rates for the coupons had to be comparable with industry norms, which couldn't happen if they weren't delivered to the stated circulation of the papers.

If the industry norm for redemption is 3 percent, and the stated circulation of a newspaper is 100,000, the anticipated number of redeemed coupon would be 3,000. But if the newspaper had an actual circulation of only 75,000, a 3 percent redemption would amount to 2,250. So even though the redemption rates were the same, clients judging the performance of our insert based upon a circulation of 100,000 would think our redemption would be 25 percent below the norm. That might be enough to make the client think our product was not worth using.

Many publishers were pleased with this program because it amounted to "found money." Many committed to distribute the inserts. The president of the National Newspaper Publishers Association, the national organization that represented the nation's black newspapers, thought the association should have been doing this program rather than a nonnewspaper entity. I even expanded the distribution by using "zoned" editions of general market newspapers in cities where it was possible to reach our target market in that manner.

But after a couple of years, we terminated the program because it was barely profitable and had slim long-term prospects of growing significantly. Building a successful business is difficult when the fate of an essential part of your marketing plan is beyond your control. Our distribution system was not going to get better because black newspapers were on the decline.

Lessons Learned Along the Way

34. Responsibility without the commensurate authority is unacceptable.

35. Do not hire or partner with a person or entity unless and until you have confirmed that the partner or entity has been thoroughly vetted.

36. Competence is as important as honesty, integrity, and commitment.

37. Don't go into business with someone devoid of financial assets, especially when the void is not offset by an invaluable skill.

Advocacy Alliances and Associations

Black Enterprise, in my opinion, has fostered black entrepreneurship more effectively than any other entity since its inception. The mission was inherent in the actions and commitment of most of the staff, especially those of us in leadership positions. Some of the management staff represented the magazine or individually participated in various industry and professional organizations. I was involved in many of these activities, but two were especially important to me: the Black Owned Communications Alliance (BOCA) and the National Association of Black Owned Broadcasters (NABOB).

The Black Owned Communications Alliance supported one of my strong beliefs that black media was not doing enough to "marshal our troops," our readers, listeners, and viewers. I believed we needed to impart more strongly the strategic role black media played in black life. We could not rely on the general media to provide us information critical to our community's growth and survival, nor could we expect it to advocate for us. I suggested we start our own advocacy effort in our own media because we controlled everything we needed to make it happen.

We convened a meeting that included Edward Lewis, publisher of *Essence*; John Procope, publisher of the *New York Amsterdam News*; Eugene Jackson, president of the National Black Network; Earl; and me.

We decided to invite Joel Martin, president of J. P. Martin Associates Inc., to join our group and have her advertising agency develop our media campaign. She created the name Black Owned Communications Alliance, and her ad campaign was award winning and highly acclaimed.

BOCA and its purpose were announced on the Publisher's Page of the December 1979 issue of *Black Enterprise* with BOCA's premier ad in the same issue. The campaign left an indelible impression on our audience and continued for several years.

The National Association of Black Owned Broadcasters is the major industry organization representing the interest of the nation's black-owned broadcasters. It was conceived by Eugene Jackson and Sidney Small, the principals of the National Black Network; Ragan Henry, owner of Broadcast Enterprises Network Inc. and owner of six radio stations; Pierre "Pepe" Sutton, president of Inner City Broadcasting Inc.; and a few other black owners. E.G.G. Dallas Broadcasting Inc. was invited to join the organization when we were purchasing our stations in the Dallas–Fort Worth metroplex.

I became active in NABOB. Initially, the primary movers and shakers of the association were a few influential owners. We worked to build influence and clout through our presence and persistence at the Federal Communication Commission (FCC) and the selection of attorney James L. Winston as NABOB's executive director. His firm specializes in broadcast law and interacts with the FCC on behalf of its clients. Jim Winston, as of this writing, is still executive director of NABOB, which is stronger and more influential than ever.

NABOB cultivated a significant relationship with congressional representatives Mickey Leland and Cardiss Collins and the Congressional Black Caucus. We testified at congressional and FCC hearings, which was crucial because the Reagan administration and its FCC chairman, Mark Fowler, had made every effort to eradicate all vestiges of affirmative action in FCC policy. NABOB is a prime example of how black entrepreneurs must work together to establish and maintain strong adversarial alliances and organizations if we are to survive and succeed in what is still a hostile environment.

Lesson Learned Along the Way
38. In business and society, it is advantageous to participate in effective adversarial organizations.

In the 1980s, we considered whether Earl G. Graves Ltd. should have a board of advisers. I thought it might be a good idea. I did not search for negative aspects of such an action. The move was implemented, and it eventually led to my departure from the company in March 1987. Fortunately, my policy of always dealing honestly and openly with Earl and maintaining my integrity regardless of consequences made our separation amicable and mutually respectful. Our friendship survived and grew stronger.

I knew most of the people Earl invited to become our advisers. But there was one prominent and successful person I did not know and who did not know me and whose distrust created a minor chasm in Earl's relationship with me. His name escapes me, so let's refer to him as Mr. D.

During my fifteen and a half years with *Black Enterprise* and Earl G. Graves Ltd., I filled many key roles, one of which was chief financial officer. My MBA concentration had been in international business, but I had taken accounting and financial courses and was proficient in finance. Using an Apple II Plus personal computer in 1981, I created the first budget ever created in house for our group of companies.

During his discussion with Earl, Mr. D discovered that I had unlimited signing authority for checks. He could not deal with the trust and confidence that Earl had bestowed upon me and urged him to limit my signing authority, which Earl eventually did. Having that financial responsibility partially diminished did not cause me to lose sleep. But having a stranger question my integrity without knowing me pissed me off. From Mr. D's perspective, it might have made a lot of sense, but I resented the inference, and I didn't like that Earl had accepted it.

I disagreed with the way Earl had gotten involved in operating the radio stations, especially with our dismissal of general manager Bill Chatman and his eventual argument and fallout with our programming consultant, Kent

Burkhardt. These actions were his right, but his knowledge of the radio business and our stations' operation and limitations were insufficient. Earl thought that if he got involved, he could fix everything, but he made matters worse.

Our relationship was eroding. I might have been wrong, but I did not believe it was my doing. Nevertheless, I continued to put forth my best to make our companies the best they could be. Although I had no ownership in Earl G. Graves Ltd., I considered it to be my company, and I functioned in that fashion.

Although I never discussed my situation with anyone, Edward Lewis, president and publisher of *Essence*, invited me to lunch. Ed had grown up in my neighborhood and Audrey had known him well, but Ed and I didn't get acquainted until I joined *Black Enterprise*. At our luncheon, he said he had heard I was looking to leave *Black Enterprise* and wanted to know if I would be interested in joining *Essence*. I said the rumor was untrue and declined his offer.

Shortly before it was announced that I was leaving *Black Enterprise*, Inner City Broadcasting's in-house counsel asked if I would be interested in running the cable system for which they had just been licensed in Queens, New York. That offer interested me, but I had already committed to the General Motors Dealer Development Academy, and I wanted to become my own boss.

My interest in owning an automobile dealership was stoked by my association with Eddie Stamps. When E.G.G. Dallas Broadcasting Inc. took control of the radio stations in Fort Worth, Texas, I called the presidents of the city's three major banks and asked for a meeting pertaining to my company doing business with them. The banks were Continental National Bank of Fort Worth (we inherited an account from them through our acquisition), the Fort Worth National Bank, and First National Bank of Fort Worth. Before I gave any of them our business, I wanted to know more about how they conducted their businesses. It was my way of showing them that I expected my company to be treated with respect and that my company would not tolerate second-class treatment.

The only bank president who met with me was James Perry from First National Bank of Fort Worth. Also attending the meeting was an assistant vice president, Eddie Stamps. Eddie was black, which answered one of my questions.

Eddie Stamps became our personal banker, and our business and personal relationship blossomed. He knew his business, took good care of me, and always came through when I needed him. We had lunch or dinner together at least once whenever I came to town. He would sometimes discuss his intentions to acquire an automobile dealership, which caught my interest. I had worked with the National Automobile Dealers Association via *Black Enterprise*, so I was familiar with the industry regarding minority dealer ownership. I decided It would be worthwhile to explore further. Eventually, I interviewed, took and passed the test for the academy, and decided, at age fifty, to begin a new business career as an automobile dealer.

I told Earl I was leaving the company, and we needed to meet to discuss my decision. I did not want him to have any questions or doubts about why I was leaving. Our business relationship was ending, but there was no enmity, from my perspective, in my departure. I felt our mutual respect was strong and that our friendship should endure. We'd spent the past fifteen years fighting the good fight side by side, and I always had his back.

When we met in his Scarsdale home, I listed each reason and incident that indicated to me that our relationship was changing for the worse. He didn't disagree with anything I said. I asked for severance pay and detailed what I thought would constitute an equitable package, and he granted all my requests.

About a week before my final work day, Earl asked me if I would postpone my appointment to the GM Dealer Development Academy until the following year. I declined because my commitment to leave was firm. In addition, I had no assurance there would be a class, or a place for me in it if there was one, the next year.

Lessons Learned Along the Way

39. A bird in the hand is worth two in the bush.

40. When you have made a well-thought-out decision, and you are comfortable with it, don't change it for someone else's benefit.

General Motors Dealer Development Academy

The General Motors Dealer Development Academy was established to increase minority ownership of GM dealerships. It recruited and trained minorities to become successful owners and operators of automobile dealerships. My class 14 assembled on April 26, 1987.

The one-year training period consisted of several four-week classroom training sessions in various departmental operations, such as new and used car sales, parts and service, and finance and insurance. Following those sessions were in-dealership phases, where we used the knowledge and theory we learned in the classroom to operate the departments we studied.

The classroom training took place in Warren, Michigan, and we lived in a Residence Inn in nearby Madison Heights. The training was intense and comprehensive. A strong comradery developed among us, which was to be expected given our common drive to succeed in our quest to become automobile store owners.

Each of us was assigned a GM division. I was assigned to the Buick division, and I trained at Mark Buick in Yonkers, New York. The owner, Mark Hermann, also lived in Chappaqua.

Our sponsor owners shared their dealerships' monthly financial performance with us. Mark agreed to share his report on the condition that he black out the bottom-line numbers. I didn't mind because if I needed to know the blacked-out figures, I could just do the math. Otherwise, Mark was as accommodating as he needed to be.

I've always maintained that 90 to 95 percent of running any business is the same or very similar from business to business. The remaining 5 to 10 percent is unique to each business. I learned the unique 5 to 10 percent of that Yonkers dealership from the department managers. They readily shared their inside knowledge, especially the used car manager and the truck manager. The truck manager, Bill Tyler, became my general manager when I bought my dealership in 1989.

The highlight of my training at the academy was when my colleagues selected me to give the Class 14 Academy Graduates Spokesman's Address. I discussed my thoughts regarding the speech's contents with my thirteen colleagues and solicited their ideas and concerns.

Graduation took place at the Westin Hotel in Detroit, Michigan, on April 28, 1988. In the speech, I focused on how we would like to see "a greater commitment from GM if the bottom line of this program—a significantly greater number of minorities who are competitive and profitable GM dealers—is going to really be in the black." I also delivered four recommendations that articulated the graduates' concerns.

My speech was a winner! It was one of the best speeches I had ever written and delivered, and I received great applause. L. E. Reuss, who was then executive vice president of the General Motors Corporation, and Joseph J. Vasquez, director of dealer business management and development, were congratulatory, as were the rest of the corporate management in attendance. I was proud of the way I represented class 14, and they were equally proud of me. The next step was to get a good deal.

Sobers Chevrolet Inc.

After completing our year of training, we were not cut loose to fend for ourselves. Joe Vasquez and his dealer business management and development department helped us find dealerships to buy. Our primary financing would be through an investment from Motors Holding Corporation, a division of General Motors Acceptance Corporation, which became our major stockholder. We were to buy them out as soon as possible and become the sole owner of our store.

Minority dealer candidates for the next class, number 15, would have a minimum financial requirement of $85,000. My class 14 financial investment was $200,000. Each academy graduate was awarded $10,000 to be used as a portion of their investment. I assembled my investment by using my savings, borrowing from my retirement funds, and receiving a significant loan from my sister.

Although I favored acquiring a deal in the northeastern US, I had been giving considerable thought to other locales. My primary alternative was North Carolina. The Carolinas were on the upswing economically, and North Carolina was more liberal than any other southern state at that time.

After visits and evaluations in New York, Massachusetts, and the Carolinas, I decided to buy a dealership in Mooresville, North Carolina. Mooresville is about thirty miles north of Charlotte, near Lake Norman, an upscale desirable area.

The deal had some drawbacks, but I was willing to take the chance that I could overcome them. US automotive sales had bottomed out, and I and many others believed the upturn was near. GM was about to release its revamped product lines, which were receiving positive praise around the industry.

My major concern was selling enough new and used cars to cover the additional expense of the previous owner's bank loan that I had assumed.

Selling used cars was more important than selling new cars because used cars represented dealership assets sitting on my lot that needed to be converted to cash.

If we sold a new car and a trade-in allowance was part of the transaction, technically, that sale was not completed. A profit could not be realized until that trade-in was sold for an equal or greater amount than we allowed for it. In addition, that sale had to cover whatever maintenance and repairs we performed on the vehicle to bring it up the standard of our sales guarantee. To increase the sale of used vehicles, I instituted a thirty-day warranty on all used-car purchases. I only got burned once, and that was on a Hyundai that I had instructed the salesman not to take in.

Long term, I wanted to relocate the dealership out toward Interstate 77, where the area's significant growth was taking place. Hotels, retail outlets, and various commercial ventures were building there or planning to do so. Twice, I was propositioned to buy land in that vicinity to fulfill that goal. But the dealership would have to be trending toward profitability for me to even attempt to entice GM to participate in such a venture. The dealership could not finance it alone.

Sobers Chevrolet was in the heart of Mooresville, 156 North Broad Street, as was a Ford dealership one block to the north and an Oldsmobile dealership one block south. The railroad spur that served local mills ran through the center of Mooresville, in front of our stores. But the real action would eventually be near Interstate 77 and Highway 150, adjacent to the Lake Norman area.

Wayne Sobers signs the official General Motors Dealership Agreement for Sobers Chevrolet Inc., January 4, 1989

If I had been superstitious, I probably would have backed out of the deal at the closing, when I discovered that the dealer number assigned to me was 66666, which I associated with the devil's number, 666. I brought it up, but given the difficulty of getting it changed, combined with the fact that I rarely allowed superstitions to govern my actions, I let it pass.

Through my connections in New York, I had been referred to a real estate agent in the Charlotte area who found me a one-bedroom apartment in a house two blocks from the dealership. It was comfortable and moderately priced. I worked long hours, so being close to the store was a benefit. I didn't expect to have visitors, except an occasional family member, so it worked for me.

Yvonne was my first visitor. She came down to spend a week with me in February and brought about six inches of snow with her. Folks in North Carolina panic when snow is forecasted and go berserk when it occurs. One of my administrative staff asked me on a Tuesday morning if she could leave early that afternoon. When I asked why, she told me she needed to prepare for the snowstorm, which was expected to be only two to three inches of accumulation and was not predicted to occur until the Friday. She was upset when I told no, and she performed in a near panic state for the following day and a half until I let her leave early on Thursday afternoon.

Yvonne and my staff helped clean snow off the cars in the lot so we could be ready for potential customers. Few appeared. I supposed they were hibernating. A few hours after the snowfall ended, the snow had melted, which was typical for that area.

While Yvonne was visiting, my realtor took us to see a few houses in Mooresville and Lake Norman. Because our house in Chappaqua was not attracting any serious buyers because of a poor housing market, we could only look. A few months later, I had Yvonne take our house off the market. I wanted to get a better perspective of how Sobers Chevrolet would fare.

My service department and body shop were excellent. Bill Tyler, who resigned from Mark Buick and became my general manager, was an experienced and trusted backup. My sales staff could have been better; they were a little deficient when it came to prospecting for clients on their own. My business manager was efficient and knowledgeable, but I was never comfortable about her commitment. Less than six months into my ownership, with no sign of the business being in difficulty, she asked if I was interested in selling the business. She knew someone who was interested in buying it. I found that incident to be insulting and negative and indicative of a person who was not a serious member of my team. From then on, I trusted her less.

When my service manager, Clark Gordon, had a heart attack while I was on vacation with my family on Fort Myers Beach, Florida, his assistant stepped up, assuring me he could handle the department and that there was no need for me to cut my vacation short. This was the same person I had passed over when I hired Clark, and he never displayed any malice to Clark or to me.

Sobers Chevrolet didn't provide any medical insurance for its employees. Nevertheless, I felt I should assist Clark. When I visited him, I told him I would pay him his full salary for one month. I would have liked to have done more, but it wasn't possible. Clark was grateful but was unable to return to work.

During the first months of my ownership, we had sold a customer a new car. This customer was a former business owner in New Jersey and had retired to North Carolina. He wanted us to return a few hundred dollars to him because the car he had purchased didn't have a certain feature. When we declined, he took us to court, and the judge threw the case out within twenty minutes.

That angered him more, and he vowed to appeal the judge's decision. My legal fees to defend against the suit were more than what he was trying to extort from us. I made a basic business decision, which galled me. I paid him what he was seeking and told him that if he ever set foot on my dealership property again, I would have him arrested for trespassing and threatening behavior.

There was another character who persisted in driving onto the property in a light truck with a confederate flag attached to the rear of his cab. He was trying to intimidate me. When my senior sales person, Duke, finally confronted him, the interloper asked, "How can you work for a black man?" Duke told him that he liked working for me and that if he ever came on the property again, he would regret it (or words to that effect). The man took Duke's message seriously and never trespassed on the property again.

Family Milestones

The period from summer 1987 through December 1989 was replete with family milestones. My emotions, focus, parenting, and leadership were tested.

My brother-in-law, Donald Hinson, had a heart attack just before Thanksgiving 1987 and died of a second attack on December 2, 1987, at age 58, while still hospitalized. I provided as much support as I could to my sister, my nephew Donald Jr., and my nieces Lori and Lisa. The youngest, Lisa, was attending Tuskegee University pursuing a doctoral degree in veterinary medicine.

Lisa was upset because Jean did not tell her that her dad had been hospitalized. She wouldn't accept the explanation that her father, believing he would recover soon, directed my sister and I not say anything. She was preparing to take her final exams, and Donald was determined not to distract her.

On the home front, my oldest son was recovering in a drug rehabilitation facility, Alpha House, in central New York State, where Lori had previously worked. Visiting him was a ten-hour round-trip drive from Chappaqua. His status was worrisome.

In spring 1989, Loren was desperate to leave Alpha House. The staff couldn't convince him to stay. He called Ben Jones, my best friend and Julian's godfather, and asked if he could come and stay with Ben at his home in Hilton Head Island, South Carolina. Ben said yes. If I had anticipated such a telephone call, I would have encouraged him to refuse Loren's request because I didn't think he was ready to leave Alpha House either. It didn't work out well, and Ben had to put him out.

My second son, Julian, graduated from high school in June 1989 and decided to attend the University of North Carolina at Charlotte. I enrolled him in a summer program called the University Transitions Opportunities Program: "A rigorous six-week summer collegiate experience, UTOP builds upon the scholastic abilities of the students through college courses and contact with university academic support services." He earned seven credits for attending. It began on July 4, 1989, his 18th birthday. I flew up to Westchester, and on July 3, we drove to Charlotte. It was good for us to be near each other as he adjusted to this new phase of his life.

With Julian's departure, Yvonne and our daughter, Stephanie, were alone in Chappaqua. Stephanie had just completed her freshman year of high school. Yvonne had started a new career as a sales associate at Macy's White Plains a few years earlier. I couldn't picture Stephanie being happy in the unsophisticated small-town environment that was Mooresville. There was little for a hip young person to do there. I would have to resolve that issue before I relocated them to North Carolina.

Making Hard Decisions

Sobers Chevrolet was struggling. The US automobile market had not yet recovered, and sales in Mooresville were dragging. The owner of the Oldsmobile dealership a block south of me, who several months earlier wanted to buy my store, was going out of business. It was time to take action.

Laying off employees has always been distasteful to me, but personnel is usually a business's biggest expense, so I started there. I laid off my finance and insurance person. When I assumed ownership of the dealership and assessed my staff, I had no qualified backup for finance and insurance, so I transferred my New York insurance licenses to North Carolina and became his backup. I also became a notary public that summer.

I also laid off two service technicians and my custodian. The latter was a single mother with a son afflicted with a swollen head. She had approached me several months earlier in dire need of a job, and the only position where I had a need was as a custodian. Though I hired her, I was reluctant because I was concerned about how people in Mooresville would perceive a young white lady cleaning the premises of a dealership owned by a black man. She was grateful for the opportunity, meager as it was. Some of the staff knew her, liked her, and were pleased that I had hired her. It hurt to let her go.

Next, I cut all the remaining staff's salaries, including mine, 10 percent. I also asked everyone to keep their own workspaces clean, and I cleaned the bathroom, which sent a clear message about my commitment. If the owner can clean the bathroom, they should extend themselves to help make the dealership a success.

That November, I reached out to a leading Charlotte megadealer to discuss a partnership. The owner perused my financials and saw the former owner's bank loan we were saddled with. He vowed to speak with Motors Holding Corporation, saying it should not have approved the loan's assumption by Sobers Chevrolet.

After that meeting, the difficult decision became easy. I would have to turn the dealership over to Motors Holding Corporation, my major and only stockholder. If I made payments on the assumed bank loan, I could not meet payroll. I had to close before the dealership was overwhelmed with debt and I wouldn't be able to survive the closing. I was fortunate to recover my entire investment and repay my sister and the loan from my retirement fund. I ended the deal a few thousand dollars ahead. Nevertheless, I felt bad for my employees, most of whom had to find new jobs.

Soon after Sobers Chevrolet closed, the megadealer I had met with partnered with one of his general managers, purchased my former franchise from Motors Holding Corporation, and reestablished out by the interstate. He had the capacity to do what needed to be done. Location is key to any retail establishment, especially an automobile dealership. My general manager, Bill Tyler, secured a position with the new ownership.

Lesson Learned Along the Way
41. When operating a small business, create or establish a backup for key positions.

Return to Chappaqua

"Thank you, Jesus, for bringing my son back to me!" my mother exclaimed when Yvonne told her I was returning home. My mom was not praying for my business to fail, but her prayers were obviously more effective than mine.

Since 1986, my dad had been a patient in the Alzheimer's ward of Morningside House, a Bronx nonsectarian nursing home, formerly affiliated with the Episcopal Diocese of New York. His memory problems began to appear in the early 1980s. When my mother needed an operation for her stomach cancer, I asked Ben to come up from Hilton Head to stay with him while she recuperated at my sister's house. My father was too difficult for my mother to manage if she was not functioning at a hundred percent. My friend, William Curry, a New York Hospital surgeon, whom she requested perform her surgery, removed two thirds of her stomach and cured her cancer.

Early on January 28, 1986, my father had an acute reaction to his medication and was nonresponsive. Ben called 911 for an ambulance, which transported him to Bronx General Hospital.

Almost simultaneously, Space Shuttle Challenger was disintegrating seventy-three seconds into its flight, killing all seven astronauts on board.

When the hospital determined that my dad's problem probably resulted from a reaction to his medication, they wanted to discharge him. But I told them there was no one at his home to care for him. They kept him for a couple of weeks until I could get him placed in a nursing home. Bishop Wetmore, suffragan bishop of the Diocese of New York, helped get him admitted to Morningside House.

My mother would take a bus to visit my father at the nursing home almost every day. Before I went to North Carolina, I could relieve her of some of that pressure. It was difficult for her when I was away, so her delight and gratitude upon my return was understandable.

When Morningside House called my mother to tell her my father was about to pass, she called me. I rushed from Chappaqua to pick her up. He died, before we got her there, on April 8, 1992. My mother was upset that she wasn't by his side when he took his final breath and felt she had let him down. I could empathize with her, but I praised her for the devotion she bestowed upon him throughout their sixty-two-year marriage. She never let him down.

Seeking Independence

After returning from North Carolina, I wanted to remain independent, to continue to be my own boss, and to be in control of my fate. I searched for opportunities that might fulfill that vision, which led me to attend a presentation by Paul Rashba. He was an independent distributor for National Safety Associates, a company that marketed its products via multilevel marketing. I was still a salesman at heart, and his presentation appealed to me, so I decided to become a part of his team.

The company's primary products were air and water filter systems. It was a time when the environment was becoming an increasing concern, especially the cleanliness of our air and water. Few of these filter systems were available to consumers in retail outlets, but water filters were cheaper than bottled water in the long run. There were no air filters comparable with National Safety Associates' products, in size, capacity, cost, or quality.

The most profitable part of multilevel marketing occurs from building a "downline," a salesforce from which salespeople receive a commission based on sales. As the leader of a downline, you need to train, assist, and motivate your corps to maximize your earnings and their earnings. To do well, you cannot lay back and expect to prosper.

To undertake that venture, I formed WayVon, which also functioned as a small business consulting company. My downline grew to more than fifty people, and I was making money, but not enough to satisfy my needs. Julian was attending college, and Stephanie's college days were approaching. Income from WayVon was stagnating, so I had to make changes.

My neighbor, Bryan Cohen, was a registered representative at Malhotra Associates, an agency of the Equitable Life Assurance Society in White Plains, New York. He was aware of my insurance background and urged me to apply for a position at his agency, as they were constantly seeking registered representatives.

I met with agency president Roger Malhotra, and he was impressed that I had been a member of the EVLICO board of directors. He offered me a position. I would have to pass my licensing exams because my previous licenses were no longer valid. I remembered most of the insurance regulations, so the exam that would be somewhat difficult would be the Series 6, the exam that would enable me to sell mutual funds. After several weeks of studying, I took the tests and passed them all. Most new agents seldom passed them all on their first attempt.

My previous working experience with the Equitable was on the highest level, as a director on one of its boards. Monetarily, it was a godsend. This second working experience with the Equitable was on the lowest professional level and, monetarily, was as important to me as my first experience fifteen years earlier.

The Equitable: A Different View

My first entrepreneurial venture back in 1964 proved I could be successful with insurance sales. I had saved enough from my sales to make a significant down payment on my first house in 1966. The difficulty I faced this time around, twenty-eight years later, was that most of my basic prospects—friends, family, associates, and others—already had, or should've had, what I was selling. I had to find new prospects.

I worked with Emilio Paoloni, who was a mentor while I was getting accustomed to insurance agency life and procedures. We worked well together, and our friendship has become a bond that I'm sure will endure the rest of our lives. I was recognized as the class leader of the Chairman's Classic fall 1992 campaign.

I made many notable sales during my tenure and continued to learn new life lessons or be reminded of some that I should have never overlooked or forgotten. On one of my sales calls, I visited a prospective client who lived in Bedford Hills, New York, about seven miles north of Chappaqua on the Harlem Line. As I started to speak, he began repeating my last name to himself. I stopped talking. When I asked if something was wrong, he said, "When I coached the St. James Episcopal Church basketball team in the Fordham section of the Bronx many years ago, there was a guy named Sobers on the St. Paul's Episcopal Church team that used to destroy us every time we played them." He was talking about me but didn't know it. This man was remembering basketball games that took place in the early 1950s, forty years earlier.

I didn't recognize him, but I remembered the games against the St. James teams. Their home court was in the church's parish hall, and their baskets seemed as big as bathtubs. I loved to play there. I hardly missed a shot! I was reluctant to tell the client he was thinking of me, fearing I might lose a potential sale. But, I thought, if he could recall my name and my exploits from forty years prior, I must have left a positive impression on him, so I told him he was remembering me.

I can't recall whether I made the sale. But the event was a reminder that we live in a small world. People you interact with remember your deeds, good or bad, long after you've forgotten them. Leaving a positive impression is important.

The most significant thing that happened to me at the Equitable was a philosophical attitudinal change. I overheard a remark from salesman Bob R. while he was making a presentation. He was a forceful speaker with an equally positive attitude. He had asked one of the participants how his day was going, and the person responded, "I'm not having a good day, but I'm hanging in there." Bob responded, "If you're just hanging in there, you're losing!"

The remarks got me thinking about "good days" and "bad days." I had always considered myself to be a person with a positive attitude. Until I was about eleven years old, I caught a lot of colds, mostly because my mom usually forced me to overdress when I went outside to play ball. I would get overheated and take off my extra sweaters after I was already sweating.

I was tired of getting so many colds and declared, "I'm not going to catch colds anymore!" Realizing what was causing me to get so many of them, I refused to wear so many layers of clothing when I went outside to play. My mom relented, and I began wearing just what was necessary to play comfortably without removing anything. After I made that adjustment, I rarely caught colds.

After hearing Bob rebuke the participant, I reflected upon my success in ending my childhood cold-catching episodes. I decided I could repeat that with other factors in my life. I declared, "I refuse to have a bad day. I will not allow them!" I have lived by that mantra ever since and discovered that all days are good, but some are just better than others.

In early 1995, I began to reassess my progress and prospects with the Equitable. I was performing well, but I wasn't earning up to my potential. I felt there had to be other management opportunities available in my employment universe, and I found the Bedford Stuyvesant Restoration Corporation.

Lessons Learned Along the Way

42. People you interact with remember your deeds, good or bad, long after you've forgotten them. Do your best to leave a positive impression.

43. There are no bad days. All days are good, but some are better than others.

STATION: GRAND CENTRAL TERMINAL

Bedford Stuyvesant Restoration Corporation

Bedford Stuyvesant Restoration Corporation (BSRC) is in the heart of the Bedford–Stuyvesant central business district of Brooklyn. The original structure on the site was a deteriorated Sheffield Farms milk bottling plant, which was transformed into a modern 417,000-square-foot complex named Restoration Plaza.

Restoration was established in 1967 with the bipartisan support of Senators Robert Kennedy and Jacob K. Javits and with the participation of local residents. It is the nation's premier community development corporation and, in 1995, was the largest landlord in Brooklyn after the City of New York. It continues to be an influential and valued Bed–Stuy institution.

When I was conducting my job search, I saw an ad for an executive director of a $2.9 million Bedford Stuyvesant community organization, which I mistakenly guessed was for a position at Restoration. At the time, I was serving on an advisory board at *Black Enterprise* and Earl G. Graves Ltd., so I asked Earl if he could help me acquire inside information about the position. As a successful alumnus of Bed–Stuy, Earl had many community contacts. He called Al Vann, another Bed–Stuy alumnus and a New York state assemblyman, who informed him that Roderick B. "Rocky" Mitchell was the president of Restoration. (I found out later that the ad that I mistakenly thought was placed by Restoration was, in fact, placed by an organization affiliated with Al Vann.) Earl contacted Rocky and recommended that he interview me for the position.

I interviewed with Roderick Mitchell, all the primary department heads, and the chairman, Charles E. Innis. On May 4, 1995, I received an offer to join the Bedford Stuyvesant Restoration Corporation as its executive vice president.

A person who was high on the list of candidates for the job, Eric Weeks, was an acquaintance of mine. He lived in Millwood, New York, the other hamlet in our town of New Castle. One morning, when we were on a train bound for Grand Central Terminal, the terminus for the Harlem Line, he asked why I was commuting into the city. When I told him I had begun working at Restoration as its executive vice president, he told me that I had beat him out for the job. He believed he was about to be selected for the position because of his financial background. He didn't appear to have any animosity toward me, but he was disappointed he hadn't gotten the position.

My appointment to Restoration was effective May 8, 1995. Emilio wished me well, as did many of my associates at the Malhotra Agency. I transferred most of my accounts to Emilio and Darwin Davis Jr. Darwin was the son of a highly regarded black executive vice president at the Equitable. I would later enlist Emilio and Darwin to provide a 401(k) program for Restoration when, after analyzing its New England Life pension plan, I realized we needed a better plan.

I learned early in my tenure that the chairman, Charles E. Inniss, had advocated the advent of my position. Rocky did not approve of it and would say or do little things later that would make his disapproval apparent to me as my involvement in BSRC deepened.

My integration into the Restoration's activities went well. I worked well with the staff, most of whom were committed to their jobs and our nonprofit's mission. I became a member of the team they could comfortably approach, and I would listen and discuss their concerns in a neutral environment. They knew I did not have an agenda and that I wanted to achieve whatever was in the institution's best interest. But I gradually began to sense that people were wary of Rocky, and it was more than because he was the boss.

I achieved milestones at BSRC using knowledge and skills from past jobs. The institution of a 401(k) plan was the most significant because I used my insurance experience to enhance the lives of all our employees. Another was using my business acquaintance with Ken Chenault, former chairman and CEO of American Express, to gain an audience with the head of the company's foundation. As a result of the meeting, I procured a multiyear grant for our Restoration Safe Haven, an after-school and Saturday educational, arts, career training, job internship, and leadership program.

The corporation had a two-thirds ownership in Restoration Pathmark, the community's only major supermarket. When we learned that Pathmark was planning to open a superstore in the newly planned Atlantic Center in downtown Brooklyn, there were concerns that our partnership with them could be financially jeopardized.

Using experience gained from operating Earl G. Graves Marketing and Research Inc., I generated a survey to determine our potential customer loss. I hired my cousin's son, a Bed–Stuy resident, and coached him on how to randomly interview customers after they checked out but before leaving the store. The resulting information was helpful in the corporation's future negotiations with Pathmark.

About a year into my tenure at Restoration, Chairman Inniss was diagnosed with cancer. When I saw him later, I was saddened. To me, the signs of imminent fatality were clear. Several months later, Inniss died, and after a period of outward respectful mourning, Rocky went into action.

He frequently bragged, "I know my board!" implying that he could manipulate the members to do his will. Of the board meetings I attended, I didn't detect any obvious mavericks among its members, except for Inniss, William C. Thompson, William C. Thompson Jr., and Albert C. Wiltshire.

In June 1997, Rocky told me that BSRC was eliminating the executive vice president position and was terminating my employment. That statement about eliminating the position was a lie. He had already told a least one of my department heads, and when I told that department head about Rocky's pronouncement, he said, "Rocky just told you? He told me several days ago." On July 17, 1997, Rocky announced via memo that the board of directors had approved Emma Jordan Simpson to assume the position.

In my opinion, his reason for getting rid of me was that it allowed him to free up funds in the budget so he could appoint an active board member, Albert Wiltshire, to a paid staff position. In March 2000, he was elected BSRC board chairman. Rocky's underhanded dealings and the actions regarding Albert Wiltshire, I'm convinced, led to his undoing and eventual departure from Restoration.

Once again, it was time for me to revise the road map for my future.

Once again, friendship, proven performance, and reputation came to the forefront as I looked for a new opportunity. I hadn't thought about the fact that I had already partially stepped across opportunity's threshold as a member of the *Black Enterprise* advisory board.

Judge Lewis Douglass of the New York State Supreme Court, a close friend to Earl and me and the first executive vice president of Earl G. Graves Ltd., knew I was no longer at Restoration. He suggested to Earl that he hire me to be director of corporate communications. Given my experience and association with the company, he thought I could hit the ground running like no one else.

Earl asked me if I wanted the job, and I accepted. We had a meeting where he updated me on the roles of his two oldest sons, Butch (Earl Graves Jr.) and Johnny. They were running the companies. Both were highly capable young men. Butch, a Harvard Business School graduate, is president and CEO, and Johnny is a lawyer and the company's corporate counsel. I didn't foresee any significant problem working with or reporting to them, although much of what I would be doing involved Earl himself. But Earl made one request, almost as an aside, that, in good conscience, I had to challenge.

He said, "Of course, if you see them doing something that's not right, you can let me know." I told him that if he expects me to work for *them*, I should not be an informer for him. That would sow distrust and destroy any sound working relationship with them. If I thought a significant event would endanger the company, I would break the chain of command and inform him. But I doubted such a situation would occur. If I questioned or was troubled by one of their actions, the proper action to take would be to address it with them directly.

It was a good conversation to have because both Butch and Johnny perceived the closeness of the relationship between Earl and me and always, I sensed, maintained a wariness about it during my two years at the company. There were things that occurred during that tenure that I took issue with and challenged in the appropriate manner. They were few, but they were significant. Some related to my dissatisfaction with how my position was used at certain events, and others related to their evaluation of my performance and the mischaracterization of who was doing what in my department.

When I assumed responsibility for the corporate communications department, I was a consultant. But because I had supervisory and managerial responsibility for the staff, legally, I had to be a company employee. Therefore, I had to relinquish my position on the advisory board, which was not a big deal. A job was better.

The department's backlog of work was huge, and getting the department to function efficiently would require hard decisions and drastic actions. Earl's dictum was that all letters written to him required a response, and there were about fifty unanswered letters with more coming in every day. An attempt to answer all of them—in addition to maintaining the basic level of work and coping with everyday activities—stymied the department's ability to function.

The solution was to start from scratch. Only letters received in the current week going forward would get a response. I reviewed the stacks to ensure that there was no critical correspondence. I answered a couple, but all the rest were archived and marked unanswered.

The department staff was capable, but we needed to reorganize our duties. One senior staff member, Sitaya Glenn, was overworked and on the verge of leaving. I reassigned her to primarily work with Earl on his daily needs, such as speaking engagements and personal public relations requirements. This decision led to a minor confrontation with Johnny. Because he didn't see anyone else working with Earl, he concluded that Sitaya was doing all the work, even though her workload had been reduced to a manageable level. I cleared up that misconception in writing. He inferred that I wasn't doing any of the heavy lifting, and I would not let that stand.

Stacy Tackie prepared customized statistical information and research that we used in all phases of our work, such as speeches, editorials, information requests from our readers, and information for presentations our sales force would use to sell our story to an agency or client. We also prepared essays and reports that were published in other media. These actions enabled *Black Enterprise* to highlight and reaffirm the magazine's selling proposition: that it was the magazine of the nation's black businessmen and women.

With Sherllisa McNeil, we gained a talented publicist. Her writing was strong, and she was versatile. Within a few months, the corporate communications department was performing excellently. My knowledge of the company's history and culture benefited our work. I could educate many of our departments about key people and events in our history that predated most of those currently employed. I also represented the company at many external events and business and association meetings.

One incident is worth noting because it might have been the precursor of a condition that would appear in Earl several years later. When addressing small or informal groups, Earl preferred to make remarks from a sheet of paper or index cards on which short statements, in the form of an outline or bullet points were highlighted. He could then improvise and deliver his speech in a manner that appeared spontaneous.

He asked me to meet and discuss a forthcoming informal address. We discussed the topic and the points he wished to cover, which I then discussed with Sherllisa. She worked on the project and met with Earl to review it and get his approval. But when she brought it back to me, I was taken aback. The remarks were in the form of a speech, and that set off alarm bells. I questioned the format, and Sherllisa assured me that she had reviewed it with Earl and that he had approved it. I acquiesced and told her to add the finishing touches. I had no reason to doubt her.

When the time to prepare for the address arrived, Earl opened the speech and was highly annoyed. He didn't recognize what Sherllisa said he had approved. I told him that Sherllisa said that she reviewed it with him and that he had approved it. I can't recall him giving me a response. He just sat down and began marking up the speech to accommodate his style. Several years later, I began to hear that he was becoming forgetful. This incident was also the beginning of my falling out of favor with Earl regarding this position. I left the company several months later, early in 2000, when Earl decided he wanted to fill the position with someone else. I remained long enough to help the new hire get situated, but his ability to use a computer was abysmal, so he didn't last long.

Earl and I remain close friends. He struggles with short-term memory loss and is aware of his problem. In every other manner, he exudes clarity and doesn't appear to have lost his wit. I pray that his condition does not deteriorate further. He is an outstanding and empathetic person whose legacy should endure for ages. I am extremely proud of the role I played and what we accomplished during my association with *Black Enterprise* and its affiliates.

Lessons Learned Along the Way
44. True friendship will survive most differences of opinion. Don't let impulsive behavior destroy it.

STATION: WHITE PLAINS

The millennium arrived. My daily commute to Grand Central Station, hopping on the subway to Bed–Stuy and later to Union Square, was finished and wasn't in any of my thoughts for the future. I was looking to downsize.

Our kids were adults, we were empty nesters, and the Chappaqua school taxes were about to obliterate my dreams of retirement. Yvonne and I pondered our options. She was still working at Macy's in White Plains, the county seat of Westchester, which was undergoing a vibrant transformation in and around the business district. We decided that a one-level condo without steps, convenient to transportation and in proximity to the White Plains business district, should be our target. I perceived that I would retire wherever we landed, so it had to be comfortable for both of us.

That vision came to fruition when we moved into our condo in White Plains in August 2000. It is one block outside the business district, and it satisfied most of our requirements. We loved and missed many things about Chappaqua, but we easily adjusted to our new life. Yvonne could walk to work, a bus stop is at our corner, and it's a short walk to the White Plains Transportation Center, where we can take the Harlem Line south to Grand Central Terminal or north to Chappaqua. The major highways are close by and easily accessible. It was right for us.

New (Ad)Ventures

I wanted to undertake another entrepreneurial venture, so I began to seek one out that would fit my budget. I came across an electronic banking business, National Bank Drafting Systems Inc., which I envisioned as a growth opportunity, but I was wrong.

Although it used an electronic technology to read checks, the action that it facilitated—businesses accepting paper checks at the point of sale—was going to evolve into paperless electronic payments. It did allow entities to electronically withdraw funds from checking accounts, but that application was new and had slow acceptance. Also, the presenter's personal approval was required at the point of sale for the merchant to legally deposit the check electronically. The system also accepted credit cards, but the function did not have a tip feature.

I had modest success among the merchants, but I attempted to snag the big sale: organizations that had large memberships. If the organization partnered with you and offered the program as a service to its members, it would minimize delinquencies, speed up collections, and increase cash flow. My benefit would be a steady stream of income because once people committed to the process, they generally stuck with it for a long time.

One of my best friends, Ken Standard, was the president of the Harvard Club, and he got me an audience with the club's financial manager. The manager seemed to be interested in the program, but I don't think he wanted to commit to the work to initiate it. If I had acquired that account, it would have been a major door opener. It would have provided me with an entrée to other college clubs. It is amazing how the acquisition or loss of one major account can lead to a business' success or failure. Getting into that business cost me $25,000, and I didn't make most of it back. I wasn't making a living at it, so I had to move on.

Lesson Learned Along the Way

45. The acquisition or loss of one major account can lead to success or failure of a business.

Teaching

While conducting another search, I pondered how I could use my experience to earn interim income. A friend suggested I explore becoming an adjunct professor in a local college. After I was separated from active duty in the navy in 1963, I had been a substitute teacher in the Mount Vernon, New York, school system while working in the Weather Bureau. But that was in elementary school and middle school. I didn't know if I could teach at the college level. Nevertheless, I knew advertising, marketing, and economics. If I was successful doing it, why couldn't I teach it?

I made a teaching presentation in front of a panel of eight educators at the Westchester Business Institute. It was well received, and they offered me an adjunct professor position. But I became suspicious when my oldest son, now going by the name Baqiy, told me he had made the dean's list when he attended there. He was not a dummy, but he wasn't dean's list material in my estimation.

The school was trying to gain accreditation and become a four-year college. That might have accounted for the college's extraordinary effort to give students good grades. The teaching staff seemed too lax in that area for me.

One student in a marketing course I was teaching was purported to be an A student. I noticed he was talkative and frequently tried to impress students and teachers alike. When I gave the class its first test, he performed miserably. If you had read the assignments, it should have been easy to get a decent grade. There was nothing tricky on the test. When I marked his paper, I gave him a 38, which I thought was generous.

The student screamed when he saw his grade, and I thought he was going to have a fit. His mother called the dean and complained. Two teachers asked how I could have given such a grade. I presented one of them the test and the student's answers and challenged him to tell me what grade he would have given. After reading the answer to the first question, he declined.

The student probably never read the assignments because all he did was write several pages of bullshit, figuring that the volume of his crap would impress me. He did not answer one question correctly. The word was out: "Don't mess with Mr. Sobers. He don't play!" One of the other teachers seemed pleased that I took teaching seriously, and she said so. She indicated that quite a few of her colleagues did not.

After that and other minor episodes, I decided to look for another school. The next semester, I found an opportunity at Mercy College. It was a revelation compared with the Westchester Business Institute, though the school did become accredited in 2003 and changed its name to the College of Westchester. I trust the college's teaching philosophy changed for the better.

At Mercy College, writing skills were paramount. Essays had to be written in acceptable and proper English. Trash was graded as trash, and students strived to improve their writing skills.

Most of my teaching assignments were in the college's satellite locations in the Bronx and Mount Vernon. Most of the students attending those locations where black and Hispanic, and they appreciated my perspectives of what obstacles they might encounter and how to overcome them. I stressed preparation and continuous knowledge acquisition. It helped that I taught a contemporary economics course that permitted me to use daily newspapers and magazines in addition to the textbook.

One student, Marta Andujar, wrote me a letter at the end of the semester saying:

"You are a good teacher. You attack every issue with each of us in class, and you motivate or push us to think." She also stated, *"You try to include each one of us in participating in the class discussion"* and that *"you do care for all of your*

students." She concluded by thanking me for teaching the course and said, "I will take advantage of what you taught me in class, in the course."

Adjunct professors, usually receive a flat fee to teach a course. It was not the type of position you could rely on for full-time employment, so I looked for additional income sources, which led me to follow up an advertisement for First Union Bank, a North Carolina–based bank that was expanding in the mid-Atlantic United States, primarily via acquisitions. Thus began my entrance into banking. It would be an interesting job for the next six years and the one from which I would finally retire.

Lesson Learned Along the Way
46. You can connect with young people when you do so with honesty, passion, and sincerity.

Banking

When I went for the interview at First Union, no managerial positions were available, so I was open to accepting a teller position. But the young human resources manager conducting the interview said he couldn't place me in a teller position with all my experience because it would be a waste of my talent and a loss for the bank. He would speak with his manager to find me a more appropriate position. I was soon hired as a roving customer relations manager.

After a month of training, I would go to one of the eight bank branches in my district and fill in for that branch's manager. Several months later, there was a minor reorganization, and another district supervisor took over. Her former district was consolidated with mine, and my responsibility expanded to thirteen branches. I was in that capacity when the assault on the World Trade Center took place on September 11, 2001.

That day, I was working in the Croton-on-Hudson branch when a customer entered the bank and exclaimed that a plane had crashed into the North Tower of the World Trade Center. I suspected something was wrong. I knew that the sky was clear because it was in my DNA to observe the weather conditions as I left home on the way to work. I also knew that the flight path for LaGuardia did not pass over the World Trade Center. With clear conditions, it would be impossible for pilots not to see the towers.

Fifteen or twenty minutes later, when the report of the second plane crashing into the South Tower came in, my suspicion was confirmed. We were attacked with commercial airliners, hijacked and used as weapons, by Al Qaeda, a militant Sunni Islamist multinational organization founded by Osama bin Laden and others in 1988.

Two other planes were also hijacked. One was crashed into the Pentagon in Northern Virginia, and the fourth was brought down, by the revolt of heroic passengers on board, in a field in western Pennsylvania.

That September First Union acquired Wachovia National Bank and became the Wachovia Corporation, one of the nation's largest financial companies. That created a new opportunity for me, one that I would have to fight for as the merger unfolded.

With the new merger came new and revised organizational entities and new pay scales. Branch managers at First Union earned almost $20,000 less than the comparable managers at Wachovia. As my fellow managers received their increases, it wasn't hard to ascertain that my pay hadn't changed. I went to the district manager to find out why, and I was not happy.

When I asked him what was going on, he told me my salary wouldn't change "because you don't have a branch." I said, "What do you mean? I've got thirteen branches!" He said, "None of them are yours." "All right, let's make one of them mine. What branches need a manager?" He told me two branches needed managers, and one of them was the Cortlandt branch. I stated I wanted to manage the Cortlandt branch and asked him, "When do I start. Next week?"

He couldn't refuse me a manager position because I had been his district's sole customer relations manager and filled the position with distinction. I often wondered what would have happened if I never came forward to claim my just reward. My new base salary increased by $22,000 a year.

The Cortlandt Financial Center was in Croton-on-Hudson, near Cortlandt Manor, just south of Peekskill, New York. It was nineteen miles north of my residence in White Plains. The staff was competent and had a strong comradery. But my initial meeting with them did not go well. My statement was misunderstood, and we got off on the wrong foot. On the other hand, they had been working under the leadership of the teller manager, Sarah Thompson, who provided strong leadership and was excellent at her job. My remarks, which were clear and simple, were perceived as a threat to the status quo. It wasn't meant that way, but that's how Sarah and her tellers perceived it.

173

I said, "I believe each of you probably perform your jobs well. However, as the financial center manager, the buck stops with me. Therefore, if I believe some changes should be made, I reserve the right to make them. In the meantime, continue doing your jobs as you have been." I made the statement because I felt it was important to establish that I was the person in charge and although I might consult with them, I didn't plan to necessarily run the office as a democracy. It had to be clear, specifically to the tellers, that Sarah was their manager, but I was the boss.

The ice wasn't broken between us until I and Gladys Oliva, my sole financial consultant, hosted our 2003 Christmas dinner for the staff, and a few of the district people who had responsibility for our branch, at a local restaurant. By that time, they had concluded that I was always considerate of their plight, would stand up for them, and would not allow customers to abuse or intimidate them, which some tried to do.

Gladys Oliva was responsible for opening accounts and selling financial products and related services to customers. Occasionally, Gladys had a few customers waiting to meet with her, and I wanted them to be serviced before they got tired of waiting and left or went to the Chase Bank across the street. If I was not busy, I would help customers who needed a service I thought I could provide, thereby reducing the customer backup. That was a mistake.

My branch functioned well, but I did not receive a good evaluation. It wasn't because of my management function. It was because of my substitute role for the financial consultant. It was not my primary job, and I didn't perform it with excellence. To improve my evaluation as the financial center manager, I curtailed my activities as a substitute financial consultant.

My regional manager took me to task during my performance review regarding my mediocre evaluation. I promised her that my next rating would improve, and it did. My next review and those that followed were excellent.

After a few years, I began to get inquiries from other banks. I had the mistaken impression that my Wachovia pension vested at ten years. A nagging voice inside of me said to check it out, and I found out, much to my surprise, that it vested at five years. I had been working there for almost four years. Accepting a position at another bank, regardless of a pay increase, would not equate to the lifetime pension I would lose by leaving. I did not plan to work long enough at another institution to qualify for a pension. I resolved to remain at Wachovia until I retired.

I received many letters from customers pertaining to my professionalism and outstanding customer service. I made certain that my supervisors got a copy of every one of them. Many of those letters I instigated. Each time a customer commended me or wanted to do something to recognize how well I serviced their needs, or even wanted to tip me, I would ask them instead to write a letter expressing their satisfaction. No one received more letters of appreciation from customers than I did. The letters substantiated the high survey evaluation I received, as well as our branch being consistently rated number one in our district. I received the maximum performance bonus in three of the four years I managed the Cortlandt branch.

I received a certificate of appreciation recognizing my five years of service with the bank. I also received a catalog from which to choose a gift. Nevertheless, it moved me to think about how much longer I would remain there and what I would do when I retired.

Lessons Learned Along the Way

47. If you have a choice, be reluctant to perform another person's job for which you will be critically evaluated.

48. Whether you work for yourself or for someone else, when someone desires to compliment your performance, work, or the like, get them to put it in writing and give it to you. Then, you can determine how to maximize it.

Millennial Life Events

In November 1996, Jean and I gave a party for my mother to celebrate her ninetieth birthday. When she addressed her guests, who ranged in age from one year to ninety years, she reminisced about raising Jean and me and how we didn't give her much trouble. I interrupted to add a key fact she left out: the four different straps she used on us, depending on the offense, when we didn't behave. She went on to say that she would like to live to be one hundred.

As we entered the 21st century, my mother was still functioning well for a ninety-four-year-old. Nevertheless, Jean and I were concerned about her living alone. Although Jean got her an emergency alert button, my mother was hesitant to wear it because she set it off accidently once, and she was upset by the emergency services responding to it. With some reluctance, she moved in with Jean.

My mother could be stubborn. She constantly fought to display and preserve her independence. Jean could also be stubborn. There were days when I'm sure that the interaction between them was like mixing oil and water. Jean installed a stairlift seat to help our mother go up and down the stairs.

In 2002, Jean had a mild stroke and had to use the stairlift as much as Momma. She had been having someone come to her house to help with the housekeeping. But after her stroke, her own needs increased, and it became difficult to ensure our mother's well-being. Jean and I decided it was in Momma's best interest to put her in a nursing home. The decision infuriated Momma, and Jean was the object of all her anger, but it was the only realistic option we had.

My aunt Muriel accompanied Jean and my mother to the Ozanam Hall of Queens Nursing Home, a short distance from Jean's house. It was a well-maintained nonprofit facility run by the Carmelite Nuns. We were all pleased with it, but Momma didn't like it. She attempted so many escapes that they posted her picture on the "rogues gallery," which was in the security booth at the facility's entrance. Many months passed before she ceased to be a potential escapee.

Jean would drive her housekeeper to Ozanam Hall and would send her up to visit Momma and check on her needs and desires. Rarely would she go up to visit herself. I suspect that she anticipated hostile vibes, but I believe Momma really would have liked to have seen her. She loved us too much to remain angry at us. On March 3, 2003, Jean moved into the Longview, an independent and assisted living facility in Ithaca, New York, where she could be near Lori, her oldest daughter who had arranged the move.

I usually visited Momma Tuesday and Thursday evenings and Saturday afternoons. On Saturday, I would frequently take her out for short drives, sometimes to the Bayside Marina; take a walk, with her in a wheelchair, around the neighborhood; or just sit out in the courtyard and talk with her.

Early in her residency at Ozanam Hall, I brought her to my house in White Plains, which she enjoyed. But she had become so acclimated to her new life that she wanted to return "home" before it was too late. During that visit to White Plains at Christmas in 2003, she met Brian, who would marry my daughter, Stephanie, on July 23, 2004. She could not attend their wedding in Massachusetts because she required too much assistance to make a trip.

The aide who took care of her at night, Juliette, was from Barbados like Momma, and they became close. I came to rely upon Juliette to keep me abreast of Momma's status.

My mother looked forward to my visits. She would frequently say to Juliette, "I love him so much, it hurts!" She would always ask, "How is Loren?" From the time of his birth mother Audrey's passing, he was always in my mother's foremost thoughts.

Before Momma entered the nursing home, we had a small gathering at my niece Lisa's house in Woodstock, Virginia, where Momma met and held my first granddaughter, her third great-grandchild, Makala Dionne Sobers. Although my second granddaughter, Julia Christine Sobers, was born six months before Momma's passing, she knew of her only through the pictures I showed her. She never got to hold her. She was so proud of their father, Julian, my second son, his wife, Katinia, and their budding family.

Momma used to say that if she ever hit the lottery, she would establish a compound where she would build a house for each of her children and grandchildren so we could all be around her.

I was standing at my desk on Saturday, June 20, 2006, when I got the call that Momma had died. She was four months and seventeen days short of her one hundredth birthday.

She had finished her breakfast and was sitting in her wheelchair with her legs crossed, outside of her room in the hallway. She went to sleep and peacefully passed. I cried. I called Yvonne and gave her the news, packed my briefcase, told the bank staff of what had occurred, and asked Sarah to take care of closing the branch.

I had spent a couple of hours visiting with Momma that previous Thursday. She had seemed confused, drifting off occasionally into semiconsciousness but periodically conversing with me. When I was leaving, I kissed her good night and told her I would return on Saturday.

Shortly after I left, she asked Juliette if I was coming to see her. Juliette told her I had just left, and she said, "Oh, he was here?" Juliette told her yes and that I would be back on Saturday.

Yvonne assisted me with the funeral arrangements. We had the funeral at St. Luke's Episcopal Church in the Bronx. The Reverend Canon Franklin Reid, assisted by my cousin, Reverend Canon Patricia Mitchell, Aunt

Muriel's daughter, presided over the service. We buried my mother in our family plot in the Cemetery of the Evergreens on the Brooklyn-Queens border. I was comforted when Aunt Muriel approached me after the funeral and said, "Your mother would be very pleased with the service and how everything went."

WayneTheCoach

One afternoon in January 2006, I heard an advertisement on CBS News Radio about becoming a professional coach. The advertiser was iPEC, the Institute for Professional Excellence in Coaching. I had coached people throughout my business career, and I felt this might be my calling. I attended a presentation hosted by iPEC's founder, Bruce D. Schneider, and some of his staff and thought this could be my retirement profession.

The training lasted a year, at the end of which I was certified as a professional coach. It was intensive, but I could pursue it while working at Wachovia. After three months, I solicited paying coaching clients as part of my training. It was ideally suited for me to make a smooth transition out of banking and into retirement.

iPEC is one of finest entities I have ever been associated with. Everything the company does is in the client's best interest. As an iPEC alumni, your association with them is in perpetuity. They're always there for you, providing opportunities for you to grow and prosper as a coach.

While at Wachovia, during a conversation with a customer, I shared that I was training to become a life and business coach. I offered her, in addition to anyone she might know, my services, while making clear my trainee status. She said she would keep my offer in mind. Later that day, I saw her in the supermarket, and she said, "I decided to take you up on your offer. How much will your sessions cost?"

I hadn't given any thought to what I would charge a potential client. I told her that because I had not yet received my certification, I would only charge her $100 a month, and she would receive one thirty-minute session each week. She agreed, and I was thrilled to have acquired my first paying client.

I worked with Linda for more than a year, and it was one of my most gratifying and successful coaching assignments. She wrote me the following:

Dear Wayne,

Over four months ago, I was paralyzed by my feeling of hopelessness. In my personal and professional life, I did a fantastic job taking care of everyone else. Through empowerment training, I have learned that the most important person in my life is—ME! I am discovering that I have all the answers to achieving my own happiness in life.

The past is the past, and the present and the future are what count. I look to the future no longer with fear and anxiety but with joyful anticipation. I am indebted to my wonderful coach and human being, Wayne Sobers, for his guidance and patience.

Thank you, Wayne!!

Linda

In addition to Linda, I acquired two more clients, both women, during my training. I continued to work with them after I received my professional certification. but my subsequent clients were not beneficiaries of my precertification fees. I built a website, www.waynethecoach.com, on which I published coaching plans, programs, and fees.

Part of my training consisted of six coaching sessions from a master coach. During one of these sessions, I chose my coaching niche: female-operated businesses and practices. That niche was suitable for me because I resonated well with women, female-owned start-ups were on the rise, and I believed that women were less likely to let their egos get in the way of achieving their goals. All my initial clients were women, which seemed to support my theory.

I achieved my certification as a professional coach in March 2007. I retired from Wachovia after six and a half years of service in September 2007. Yvonne retired from Macy's in September 2009. A new and interesting life was ahead of us.

The Future Unfolds

WayneTheCoach progressed well. Interacting with so many aspiring, determined, and interesting clients inspired me to excel. It is gratifying to coach people and watch them realize they can shape and control much of their own future and that their dreams are achievable.

Among my business clients were an artist, the president of a business services company, an attorney, and a coach. Among my life coaching clients were a freelance illustrator, a teacher, and a school financial administrator. One thing I learned about business coaching was that clients' personal lives were often intertwined with their business activity.

Working with so many clients who shared their dreams and aspirations with me heightened my own concerns regarding my granddaughters' futures. In September 2009, our third granddaughter, Cayden Barrett Shacochis, was born to Stephanie and Brian. Yvonne and I feel blessed to have three bright, healthy, and loving granddaughters, and they are blessed to have loving and caring parents and grandparents. Cayden was the fifth great-grandchild of Grandpa Fritz, Brian's grandfather. He was thrilled to have the opportunity to hold her alongside Makala and Julia on Christmas Day 2009.

Yvonne and I will never forget the comforting and reassuring words Grandpa Fritz shared with us when we were leaving to go home a few days after Brian and Stephanie's wedding: "Don't worry about your daughter. We'll take very good care of her." He may have sensed that we might have had some apprehension about our daughter becoming an integral part of a white family, but we didn't. We had met Brian's parents and found them, like Brian, to be wonderful.

We were happy when Brian's parents, Norm and Eileen, and two of their close friends, Janis and Carol, joined Yvonne and I on a cruise to Alaska in July 2009. I had planned it to be a celebration of our family wedding anniversaries. Yvonne and I were celebrating forty years, Julian and Tina were celebrating fifteen years, and Brian and Stephanie were celebrating five years. But Stephanie's doctor advised her not to make the trip because she was seven months pregnant with Cayden.

Seventeen of us cruised, including my sons, my daughter-in-law, and two granddaughters; Aunt Muriel, her daughter Patricia Mitchell and granddaughter Andrea Mitchell; my niece, Lisa; and two of my oldest son's cousins, Cheryl and Gloria. With Pat presiding, Yvonne and I, along with Julian and Tina, renewed our wedding vows.

We chose a Holland America cruise line sailing round-trip from Vancouver, British Columbia, Canada, so Yvonne and I could visit some of her family members in the Vancouver area and in Washington State.

Andrea and Jamel married in the homeland of our ancestors, Barbados. That event precipitated the first Sobers family reunion in Barbados in August 2012. It was attended by nearly sixty descendants of my grandmother, Florence Sobers, who was born there in September 1883. She married James Augustus Sobers in December 1906.

My nephew, Donald Hinson, our family historian, has traced the Sobers family ancestry back to Samuel William Sober—Sober being the original family name—somewhere around 1820. Cousin Rhonda James, with the assistance of Donald, created a marvelous compendium entitled "The Sobers Family 1800's–2012, Back to Our Roots" that chronicles nine generations of Sobers family members.

One of our greatest and most satisfying life events took place in the summer of 2016. It began when we attended the surprise forty-fifth birthday party for Julian in Charlotte. He was moved to the point of tears when, soon after his arrival, he turned around and saw Dale Chappelle, his first childhood friend whom he met at age three, waiting to embrace him. Dale and his wife, Davia, had flown down from Westchester County to share that event with us.

We left Charlotte with our granddaughters Makala and Julia, who would accompany us for the entire summer.

The girls took two weeks of swimming classes at the State University of New York at Purchase. We showed them the house in the Bronx where we lived before we moved to Chappaqua, and Stephanie and Cayden joined us for a weekend.

We attended the Church of St. Mary the Virgin in Chappaqua, which Yvonne and I still attend, one Sunday in July. It was the church where Julian and Stephanie were confirmed, and that was the first time Yvonne, Stephanie, me, and all our granddaughters had attended church together.

We took them on a tour of the Cemetery of the Evergreens, where fifteen of our relatives are buried. And we attended the funeral of my cousin Stephen A. Sobers Jr., who passed away and was buried on July 26, 2016.

We traveled to Toronto, where they met their ninety-four-year-old great-grandmother, Elmozine Spence, and several of Yvonne's nieces, nephews, and cousins. We stayed with Yvonne's sister-in-law, Margaret Barrett, in Scarborough, Ontario.

On the way to Toronto, we visited Jean in Ithaca. Lori met us at the Longview. Julia had been less than a year old and Makala had been six when they last saw Jean and Lori. On our return from Toronto, we stopped at Niagara Falls and then went to Seneca Falls, New York. We toured the Women's Rights National Historical Park, which tells the story of the first Women's Rights Convention held in Seneca Falls in July 1848.

We also took a boat ride around Manhattan and visited parks in Westchester County. Because Makala was a member of the junior ROTC at her high school, we took her on a tour of the US Military Academy at West Point.

The final event of their summer with us was an Auto Train roundtrip between Lorton, Virginia, and Sanford, Florida, from where we drove to our time-share at the Casa Ybel Resort on Sanibel Island, Florida. We spent two relaxing and fun-filled weeks. Julian and Tina joined us for the first week.

While in Florida, we visited Yvonne's relatives in the Fort Lauderdale area and attended a birthday party for Marjorie Stephenson, the wife of Yvonne's cousin Louis. The girls met a host of other family and friends, some for the first time.

In Virginia, when the girls left with their father after being with us for two months, sadness enveloped us. The time they spent with us was delightful! We knew it was unlikely to be replicated, so we were thankful to have had the experience. Makala said that it was the best summer they had ever had, and Yvonne and I agreed that it was also one of our best.

Lesson Learned Along the Way

49. Happiness is not having what you want. It is wanting what you have!

List of Lessons Learned Along the Way

1. Being observant will heighten your awareness and ability to learn.
2. Always be alert and aware of your surroundings.
3. Stand up for yourself.
4. Turn excitement into positive energy.
5. You've got to show up to defend your rights and the rights of loved ones.
6. A positive environment is instrumental for academic achievement.
7. Focus is essential for success.
8. Evaluate intelligence on more than school grades.
9. Be aware of politics going on behind your back.
10. Always determine the ground rules in advance.
11. Interpret unsolicited advice thoughtfully, and evaluate the motives of the advice giver.
12. Study an extra hour a day. It can improve your class standing and enhance your knowledge base.
13. You must learn *how* to learn.
14. Perform at *your* maximum capability, not in relation to your peers.
15. Be careful how, when, and why you use medication.
16. Think ahead. Visualize your future.
17. Your ego can destroy you. Keep it in check.
18. Try to recognize your deficiencies. Correct them if possible.
19. Don't be a smart ass. Be receptive to advice from those who know.
20. When involved with children, expect the unexpected. They will find trouble.
21. The only priceless possession we have is our health.
22. When logic is foggy, follow your instincts, trust your gut!
23. An influential advocate is a great asset and worth cultivating.
24. When trying something new, test it first.
25. You can't advance in life unless you're willing to take reasonable risks.
26. A strong team is an asset. Don't be reluctant to ask a teammate for assistance.
27. If you need to use a bat to get someone's attention, wrap it in cotton first.
28. Cherish the love and support you receive from others. Reciprocate it, and do not take it for granted.

29. Don't burn your bridges behind you. You may need to cross them again.
30. Plan your work meticulously and pace yourself accordingly. "Rome was not built in a day."
31. You should be ready to go the extra mile to accomplish your task and achieve your goal.
32. You can't get the business if you don't clearly ask for the order.
33. Look for opportunities that facilitate connecting and empathizing with the people you interact with. It can open doors for you.
34. Responsibility without the commensurate authority is unacceptable.
35. Do not hire or partner with a person or entity unless and until you have confirmed that the partner or entity has been thoroughly vetted.
36. Competence is as important as honesty, integrity, and commitment.
37. Don't go into business with someone devoid of financial assets, especially when the void is not offset by an invaluable skill.
38. In business and society, it is advantageous to participate in effective adversarial organizations.
39. A bird in the hand is worth two in the bush.
40. When you have made a well-thought-out decision, and you are comfortable with it, don't change it for someone else's benefit.
41. When operating a small business, create or establish a backup for key positions.
42. People you interact with remember your deeds, good or bad, long after you've forgotten them. Do your best to leave a positive impression.
43. There are no bad days. All days are good, but some are better than others.
44. True friendship will survive most differences of opinion. Don't let impulsive behavior destroy it.
45. The acquisition or loss of one major account can lead to success or failure of a business.
46. You can connect with young people when you do so with honesty, passion, and sincerity.
47. If you have a choice, be reluctant to perform another person's job for which you will be critically evaluated.

48. Whether you work for yourself or for someone else, when someone desires to compliment your performance, work, or the like, get them to put it in writing and give it to you. Then, you can determine how to maximize it.
49. Happiness is not having what you want. It is wanting what you have!

Made in the USA
Middletown, DE
27 January 2020